Making Sense of
English in
the Law

English in Use Series
General Editor: David Crystal

Making Sense of
English in
the Law

Martin Cutts

Chambers

EDINBURGH   NEW YORK

Published 1992 by W & R Chambers Ltd
43–45 Annandale Street, Edinburgh EH7 4AZ
95 Madison Avenue, New York N.Y. 10016

A catalogue record for this book is available from the
British Library

ISBN 0–550–18038–9

Typeset by Buccleuch Printers Ltd., Hawick, Scotland.
Printed in England by Clays Ltd., St. Ives plc.

Preface

Law is all about the meaning of words. A friend of mine recently became entangled in a tricky court case. Immediately he was awash with the language of the law: affidavits, pleadings, easements, bailments, injunctions and interlocutories. Even simple black-and-white words he thought he understood, like 'land', seemed to take on a shade of grey when lawyers used them, worsening that feeling of powerlessness which anyone who has ever been on the wrong end of a legal action will recognize.

Without a rough idea of what law language means, you're at a disadvantage if you have a legal problem. All of us as citizens are deemed—that's a word defined in the book—to know the law, thousands of pages of it, paragraph by paragraph. This is a legal fiction—another defined term—but it's at the root of an important maxim, that ignorance of the law is no excuse. In other words, if you offend unwittingly against the civil or criminal law, you are as much to blame as someone who offends knowingly. Most people have a rough idea of the main features of the criminal law, but the civil law, concerned with shopping, housing, contracts etc, is complicated and full of terms which are rare in everyday speech.

This book doesn't tell you everything you need to know and doesn't aim to give specific guidance on any legal case you may be involved in. But it should prove a useful starting point for your enquiries, whether you're just going to discuss the making of a will with your solicitor or take out a summons in the county court.

Naturally, any conversation you have with a solicitor will be held in the English of the late 20th century. Yet a legal document drawn up by the same solicitor, or a consumer contract you sign in a shop, could well be written in a strange mixture of medieval and modern language. Words extinct in the common tongue, like 'expiration' and 'effluxion', find a last refuge in these documents, to the confusion of non-lawyers.

Preface

It is true there are certain 'terms of art' which lawyers need. They are a useful shorthand, part of the specialized language which every industry or profession uses to communicate among its own members—terms like 'Mareva', 'distress', 'diligence', 'negligence' and 'duty of care'. But many words traditionally considered terms of art are merely legal flavouring, like 'hereof', 'hereto', 'hereinafter', 'thereof', 'thereto', and 'aforesaid'. Such words have no special meaning; lawyers can, if they wish, replace them with the modern equivalents given in this book.

Similarly, the long unpunctuated sentences favoured by lawyers can be chopped into shorter ones or broken down into lists without sacrificing accuracy or precision. As one professor of law said, the only solution to the problem of long sentences is to say less and use full stops more. And the story that legal documents must not be punctuated is simply untrue. If it were true, every Act of Parliament would be unlawful.

Some lawyers already agree that their use of language must be improved, banding together to fight for plain language in their profession, and some judges are renowned for the clarity of their judgments in complicated cases. Public reports of judges' decisions in important cases, written by barristers and checked by the judges themselves, are often admirably clear and concise. In the last few years, the clarity of language and layout has improved in legal documents like insurance policies. So it can be done.

The training of lawyers in writing and other communication skills is at fault. Many receive little or no instruction in how to draft understandable leases or letters to clients. As a result, young lawyers tend to copy how their seniors write—indeed their seniors often force them to follow the same turgid and unreadable style. Thus, by each successive generation of lawyers, the public is sold the ancient myth that legal writing must always be full of gobbledygook.

The more people know that this myth is without foundation, the less likely lawyers are to get away with perpetuating it. And the more people know about the language of the law, the better they will understand their lawyers' advice and be able to take informed decisions on it. I hope this book will help in both respects.

English in Law gives information about the law of England and Wales as I understand it at October 1991, together with definitions of many common Scots law terms.

I am grateful for the help of Judith Philip, who commented on certain entries concerning EC law, and Amanda Petrucci, who commented on entries concerning Scots law.

Martin Cutts

Pronunciation Guide

Vowels

i:	need	/ni:d/
ɪ	pit	/pɪt/
i	very	/'vɛri/
ɛ	pet	/pɛt/
æ	pat	/pæt/
ʌ	other	/'ʌðəʳ/
ʊ	book	/bʊk/
u:	too	/tu:/
u	influence	/'ɪnfluəns/
ɒ	cough	/kɒf/
ɔ:	ought	/ɔ:t/
ɜ:	work	/wɜ:k/
ə	another	/ən'ʌðəʳ/
ɑ:	part	/pɑ:t/

Glides

eɪ	plate	/pleɪt/
aɪ	sigh	/saɪ/
ɔɪ	ploy	/plɔɪ/
oʊ	go	/goʊ/
aʊ	now	/naʊ/
ɪə	hear	/hɪəʳ/
ɛə	fair	/fɛəʳ/
ʊə	poor	/pʊəʳ/

Consonants

p	pit	/pɪt/
b	bit	/bɪt/
t	ten	/tɛn/
d	den	/dɛn/
k	cap	/kæp/
g	gap	/gæp/
ʃ	shin	/ʃɪn/
ʒ	pleasure	/'plɛʒəʳ/
tʃ	chin	/tʃɪn/
dʒ	budge	/bʌdʒ/
h	hit	/hɪt/
f	fit	/fɪt/
v	very	/'vɛri/
θ	thin	/θɪn/
ð	then	/ðɛn/
s	sin	/sɪn/
z	zones	/zoʊnz/
m	meat	/mi:t/
n	knit	/nɪt/
ŋ	sing	/sɪŋ/
l	line	/laɪn/
r	rid	/rɪd/
j	yet	/jɛt/
w	quick	/kwɪk/

ʳ indicates an 'r' pronounced only before a following vowel
' precedes the syllable with primary stress

Guide to Readers

Bold type, eg **assault** at **battery, offence** at **false accounting,** or **property** under **restitution,** is used to refer the reader to other entries in the book.

A

abandonment

1 The **offence** by a parent or **guardian** of leaving a **child** under 16 to look after itself without adequate care and protection. A **court** may allow such a child to be adopted without its parents' consent.

2 The giving up of a legal right. This would include the abandonment of a mortgaged property to the lender or of rented property to the landlord.

3 The giving up of an **action** by a **plaintiff** or **pursuer,** or the giving up of an **appeal** by someone found guilty of a crime.

abatement of nuisance

Bringing to an end or destroying the cause of a **nuisance** by the individual who is being annoyed: a form of self-help. Someone seeking to end a nuisance must not do more damage than is necessary, and would be unwise to enter someone else's property for this purpose without giving **notice** to the owner.

abduction

Taking away without consent a **person,** such as a wife from a husband, or a **child** from its parent or **guardian.** It is an **offence** to take a child from someone's lawful **custody** without authority or good excuse.

abode, place of

Where someone usually lives.

abortion

Terminating a pregnancy by miscarriage or the expulsion of a fetus before the pregnancy reaches its full term. Doctors in England, Scotland and Wales can lawfully perform an abortion during the first 24 weeks of pregnancy if:

1 the mother's life would be at risk if the pregnancy continued; or

2 her (or her children's) physical or mental health would be at risk if the pregnancy continued; or

3 there is substantial risk of the **child** being born with a serious abnormality.

The consent of two doctors must be obtained. Unless the mother's life is at risk, doctors and nurses may refuse to take part in an abortion on grounds of conscience. A husband (or partner) has no legal right to prevent his wife having an abortion. A girl under the age of 16 needs parental consent to an abortion, though a **court** can override parental refusal if it is satisfied that abortion is in the best interests of the girl. Girls under 16 may not normally be given advice or treatment on contraception or abortion without parental consent. Abortion is illegal in Northern Ireland except when the mother's life is at risk.

absolute discharge

A **Crown Court** or **magistrates' court** decision that a **guilty** individual should not be punished. It is, nevertheless, a **conviction** and can be appealed against. **Courts** sometimes give an absolute discharge if they think the police should have turned a blind eye to the **offence** (for example, when the driver of a fire engine goes through a red traffic light on the way to an emergency). The decision does not bring a previous **suspended sentence** into effect.

absolute discretion

Complete freedom to act. Often called, in long-winded *legalese, absolute discretion without the necessity of obtaining any consent.*

absolvitor

In Scots law, **judgment** in favour of the **defender**.

abstracting electricity

The **offence** of dishonestly using, wasting or diverting electricity. In Scots law the offence is also covered by the **common law** of **theft**.

ACAS

The Advisory, Conciliation and Arbitration Service, a **statutory body** which promotes the improvement of industrial relations and collective bargaining between **trade unions** and employers. ACAS, at the request of one or more of the **parties,** can offer help in **trade disputes** and help the parties in an **industrial tribunal case** to reach a **settlement.**

accessory

Someone who successfully incites another to commit a **crime** or who helps him or her to do so.

accomplice

Someone who helps to commit a crime or is an **accessory** to it.

accord and satisfaction

A **creditor's** acceptance of an agreement suggested by the **debtor,** which satisfies the debt and so prevents the creditor suing the debtor.

account of profits

See **tort.**

accused

The individual alleged by the **prosecution** to have committed a **crime.**

acquittal

A **court** decision that the **accused** is **not guilty.**

acknowledgement of service

A document, accompanying a **writ** (sense 1), which a **defendant** should return to the **court** on receiving the writ.

act

To perform the duties of a **solicitor,** as in *We act for Mr Grumble in this matter.*

action

A legal proceeding in the **civil courts**.

act of God

An extraordinary event or circumstance, such as an earthquake or hurricane, which directly causes an accident and could not have been foreseen and guarded against. **Insurance policies** sometimes do not provide cover against their effects. A gust of wind which directly causes a car to veer off the road is an act of God, but heavy rain or fog which drivers respond to inappropriately, causing an accident, is not. Claiming that an event is an act of God is now a rare **defence**.

Act of Parliament

A document setting out the **law;** normally it has been passed by the **House of Commons** and **House of Lords**. Modern Acts begin with a long title which summarizes their aims, and end with a short title which can be easily quoted in other documents.

See **interpretation; Parliament.**

Acts of Adjournal

In Scots law, procedural regulations made by the High Court of Justiciary.

Acts of Sederunt

In Scots law, procedural rules made by **judges** in the **Court of Session**. They are recorded in the Books of Sederunt.

actus reus

[Latin: prohibited act] For someone to have committed a **crime** they must be proved to have satisfied two tests: the actus reus and the **mens rea** (intention). For example, **rape** consists of an actus reus (unlawful **sexual intercourse** by a man with a woman without the woman's consent) and a mens rea (knowledge that the woman did not consent). Unless both tests are satisfied, the **jury** must acquit. In some **offences**, however, the **court** regards the committing of the offence as sufficient proof of guilt—intention is assumed. These are called **strict liability** offences.

address for service
See **service**.

ad idem
[Latin: towards the same] Agreement on a point between, say, opposing **barristers**, or between **parties** as to what terms should be included in a **contract**.

adjournment
The postponement of a **court** or **tribunal hearing**. This may be to a fixed date or indefinitely.

ad litem
See **guardian ad litem**.

administration order
A method which a **debtor** can use to make a single payment regularly into the **county court** office which shares it equally among his or her **creditors**; they cannot then pursue the debtor for their money. The order can be used for total debts below £5 000, though this is to change in 1993.

administrative law
The body of **law** relating to the administrative powers of central and local government. **Courts** can examine the use of such powers on legal but not policy grounds.

Admiralty Court
An English **court**, part of the **Queen's Bench Division** of the **High Court**, which deals with maritime claims in **civil law**, such as **salvage**. In Scotland, similar matters are disposed of by the **Court of Session**.

adopted as holograph
In Scots law, a statement in the signatory's handwriting at the end of certain kinds of **deed** which says that although the deed is not in the signatory's handwriting, the signatory regards it as being so. The deed is then valid without having to be witnessed.

adoption

A procedure in which a **civil court** makes an order giving **parental responsibility** over a minor to someone other than its natural parents. On adoption, the minor becomes the legal child of its adoptive parents. In Scotland, a child over 12 years old must give consent to adoption unless unable to do so, while a child over 16 must always give consent.

ad rem

[Latin: to the matter) This indicates that a decision or statement has a general significance not confined to the **case** in question.

adversarial (accusatorial) procedure

The system of criminal trial in England and Wales in which the **prosecution** presents a **case** against a **defendant,** the **defence** tries to undermine and demolish the case, and the **judge** acts as impartial umpire. Very little of importance is decided before the trial starts and the outcome may hinge on the performance of each side's **advocate.**

The French system, known as *inquisitorial*, differs in that, when a serious **crime** is committed, an examining magistrate, usually a junior judge, has wide powers to collect and weigh **evidence** for and against a suspect before deciding whether to prosecute. In theory this means that an independent mind studies the evidence in an attempt to weed out flimsy cases. The examining magistrate takes no part in the trial. Scottish procedure shares some characteristics of the French.

The adversarial system is used in English **civil cases**, though family proceedings involving children have abandoned it in favour of reaching a consensus in the best interests of the children.

See **procurator fiscal**.

advocate

In Scotland, a member of the Scottish **Bar** and a **lawyer** who practises. The term is equivalent to **barrister** in England, though it could apply to a **solicitor** who is a member of the Society of Advocates in Aberdeen.

affidavit

A written **statement** to be used as **evidence** in **court** proceedings. The individual making the affidavit *swears* or *affirms* that it is true before a **commissioner for oaths**, court official or **solicitor** (who must not be his or her own solicitor). In Scotland, the solicitor must be a **notary public**. A deliberately false statement in an affidavit is **perjury.**

affiliation and aliment

In Scotland, an order of the **sheriff court** or **Court of Session** declaring someone to be the father of a **child** and providing for the child's **maintenance.**

affiliation order

A **magistrates' court** order compelling a man alleged to be the father of an **illegitimate child** to make payments towards its upkeep.

affinity

A relationship by **marriage.** Countries generally have rules prohibiting marriage between certain people where there is an affinity, for example between parents and step-children.

See **prohibited degrees of relationship.**

affirm

See **oath.**

affray

The **offence** of using or threatening violence (but not by words alone). In Scotland the offence is covered by **breach of the peace.**

aforementioned

A reference to something already mentioned, as in *If the policyholder has any of the aforementioned medical conditions, the policy does not cover her for an event arising from that condition.* In such writing it is clearer and more precise to put *these* instead of *the aforementioned* or to specify in which paragraph the conditions are listed.

aforesaid

A reference to something already mentioned. Careful **lawyers** avoid it as being redundant and imprecise. For example, a document might mention the location of a house as *65 Cork Street, Middlesbrough in the county of Cleveland aforesaid.* The last word is redundant since no other Cleveland is in question.

See **said**.

age of consent

The age (16 or, in Northern Ireland, 17) at which a girl can legally consent to **sexual intercourse** or to some other act that would otherwise amount to **indecent assault**.

In England and Wales, men and women must be at least 16 before they can marry. Between the ages of 16 and 18 everybody (except a widow or widower) requires consent to marry, usually from a parent. If this is refused, a **court** may give consent. In Scotland, consent of a parent is not required after age 16.

age of responsibility

In England and Wales, under the age of 10 a **child** is regarded as *doli incapax* (Latin: incapable of committing a **crime**) and will not be charged. **Care** proceedings can be brought if the child's parents cannot or will not exercise control. In Scotland, children under 8 cannot be **guilty** of a crime. Children from 8–16 may only be prosecuted on the instruction of the **Lord Advocate,** otherwise the Children's Hearing system is used.

See **children in care**.

agency

The relationship existing where one **person**, the *principal*, authorizes another person, the agent, to act on his or her behalf in a transaction with a **third party**. The agent creates a legal relationship between the principal and the third party.

aid and abet

To help in a **crime**, while it is being committed or beforehand.

alibi

[Latin: elsewhere] If you say you were elsewhere when the **offence** was committed, that's your alibi. Before a **Crown Court** trial, you must give the **prosecution** plenty of warning of your alibi so that they have time to check it, but you can call **witnesses** in support.

In one case in 1974, Luke Dougherty was accused of **theft** but said that on the day of the **crime** he was miles away on a coach outing. His **defence** called two witnesses who were unconvincing under questioning and Dougherty was convicted because two shop assistants identified him as the thief. After nine months in prison his alibi was proved correct and he was released.

alien

Someone who is not a citizen of the state. In the UK, aliens may hold most kinds of property but may not vote or hold public office.

aliment

In Scotland, *interim aliment* is money agreed or ordered to be paid to a **child** or **marriage** partner during divorce proceedings. Payments after the divorce decree are called **periodical allowance**; if there are no divorce proceedings, they are known as aliment.

alimony

See **maintenance**.

allenarly

A Scots term for *only*, which is important when associated with a **liferent** as it prevents the liferent being regarded as a **fee**.

All ER

See **Law Reports**.

all that land

Legalese for *all the land*.

amicus curiae

[Latin: friend of the court] A **lawyer** appointed in certain **cases** to help the **court** by putting arguments in support of an interest that might not be adequately represented by the **parties** to the case, such as the public interest.

ancient lights

A landowner's right to have sunlight enter his or her windows. The right may be acquired by written agreement or by at least 20 years' continuous use. Structures which interfere with ancient lights cannot normally be erected. However, a **court** would take into account how much light the landowner needed for the **property's** normal use. Ancient lights does not give a right to protect a view. Similar rules apply in Scotland.

See **easement; light or prospect.**

ancillary relief

In **divorce** and separation proceedings, **court** orders concerning money and **property**.

annulment

A **court** declaration of nullity of **marriage.** A null marriage is one that has never been valid, for example because it was between people within the **prohibited degrees of relationship.** In all cases except non-consummation (failure to have **sexual intercourse**), annulment can only occur within 3 years of the date of the marriage.

answer

A written **pleading** given to the **court** in reply to a **claim.**

Anton Piller

In English **civil** actions, a powerful **High Court** order, named after a German manufacturing company which was among the first to get such an order. A **plaintiff** obtains it from a **judge** in secret without notifying the **defendant**. It acts as a **search warrant**, permitting entry and search of the defendant's home or business to obtain disclosure of confidential information that may otherwise be concealed or destroyed to frustrate the plaintiff's claim for **damages.**

Anton Pillers are used in cases of copyright and **trade mark** infringement and even in **divorce** actions. **Lawyers** describe them as nuclear weapons because of their shock value. Following abuse of the procedure, rules imposed in 1992 require orders to be served only during normal working hours. Defendants are allowed to take immediate legal advice, perhaps by telephone. If they refuse entry and search they can be fined or imprisoned for **contempt of court**. If they also destroy or dispose of the information sought, they can be penalized for that too.

Various legal moves are theoretically open to a defendant at the outset, including the right to have the order set aside if the plaintiff has failed to disclose relevant facts or has lied in his or her statement to the judge. But in complicated **litigation** like this, the defendant needs competent legal advice and a deep pocket. Fortunately, Piller orders are rare.

appeal

A complaint to a superior court of an injustice done by an inferior one.

In England and Wales, after a criminal trial in a **magistrates' court**, two main appeal routes are available. First, convicted people can appeal against conviction or **sentence** to the **Crown Court**, perhaps because they feel insufficient **evidence** was put forward or that the **magistrate** interpreted the facts wrongly, or that the sentence was too harsh. The Crown Court fully rehears the **case** and imposes a new decision; it may even decide to increase the sentence. Second, the convicted person or the **prosecution** may appeal on a point of law (how the law should be applied or interpreted) to the **High Court**.

Guilt in a Crown Court criminal trial is decided by a **jury**; this is more difficult to appeal against because the jury give no reason for their decision. So appeals are usually based on claims that:

1 there was some irregularity during the trial (in one case a judge pressed a jury to reach a **verdict** prematurely);

2 the judge's **summing-up** misled the jury or failed to explain things properly to them;

3 fresh evidence has been unearthed which would make the conviction unsafe and unsatisfactory—but it is unusual for fresh evidence to be allowed.

Faced with fresh evidence, the appeal court may consider what the jury's verdict would have been had they heard it.

Appeal courts in most Commonwealth countries, as well as Scotland and Northern Ireland, have wider powers to order a retrial than in England and Wales.

If the prosecution thinks a judge's sentence is too lenient, it can ask the appeal court to increase it. The prosecution cannot appeal against a verdict.

Lawyers who intend to appeal on their clients' behalf must apply for a **stay of execution** on the sentence; they often forget.

Shortcomings in the appeal system were revealed in the case of six men convicted of murdering 21 people in a Birmingham public house in 1975; they served 16 years in prison. Evidence that the police and **forensic scientists** had distorted the truth throughout the trial was ignored by judges in various appeal **hearings**, until finally the sentences were overturned in 1991.

Incompetence by an **accused's** legal representatives is not grounds for appeal.

In **civil cases**, an appeal may concern a point of **law** or the amount of **damages**.

In Scotland, the appeals system is similar to that outlined here, though of course the courts bear different names.

See **Court of Appeal**; **reclaiming motion**.

appearance

In Scots law, a **defender's** assertion that he or she will defend the **claim**.

appellant

One who appeals against a **court's decision**.

applying the proviso

In English criminal **appeal** procedure, the **court's** use of a power given by section 2 of the Criminal Appeal Act 1968. This enables the court to concede the **appellant's** point but to dismiss the appeal because the point does not constitute a **miscarriage of justice**.

apprehend
In Scots law, to **arrest** in a criminal sense.

appurtenant
Relating or belonging to.

appurtenances
A right or **interest** which accompanies the **title** when **land** is transferred.

arbitration
The settlement of a dispute by reference to an independent **party**, an **arbitrator**, appointed by the parties.

arrest
In England and Wales, the stopping and detaining of someone suspected of a criminal **offence**. Most arrests are carried out by the police. Someone wrongly arrested may bring a **civil** action for *false imprisonment*. Arrests may be made for serious offences without a **warrant** (**serious arrestable offences**), whereas arrests for minor offences usually need a warrant. *Arrestable offences* include those for which someone not previously convicted might be imprisoned for 5 years or more, such as **burglary, theft,** criminal damage, **rape** and unlawful possession of drugs, and lesser offences such as **indecent assault** on a female, corruption or smuggling.

See **citizen's arrest**.

arrestment
In Scots law, the seeking by a **creditor** of payment of a debt out of money or **moveable property** belonging to the **debtor** but held by a **third party**.

13

arrestment to found jurisdiction

In Scots law, a **court** order which stops a **defender** shifting **moveable property** (such as money or a ship) out of the court's area of **jurisdiction**. This enables the court to try the **case**.

arson

The unlawful destruction of, or damage to, **property** by fire.

articled clerk

See **trainee solicitor**.

articles of association

A document showing the regulations for the management of a company (usually a **limited liability company**) registered with the Companies Registry.

articles of roup

/raʊp/

In Scots law, the conditions of a sale by auction.

as accords of law

Scots **legalese** for *in accordance with law*—usually shortened to *as accords*.

ass

A much misquoted definition of the **law**. In Charles Dickens' 'Oliver Twist', Mr Bumble remarks: 'If the law supposes that, the law is a ass—a idiot.' Dickens may have been remembering a line from George Chapman's 17th century play 'Revenge for Honour': 'I am ashamed the law is such an ass.'

assault

Causing someone to fear, reasonably, an immediate **battery**. Bodily contact is not an essential ingredient of assault: spitting in someone's face or shaking a fist in their face may suffice.

assignment

The transfer of some legal right to another **person**. For example, a **creditor** might assign a debt to a factoring company at a discount price, and the **factors** will collect it from the

debtor at whatever price they can get. In Scots law the equivalent term is *assignation*.

assize

In Scots law, an unusual term for **jury**.

Assizes or Assize Court

A **court** in England and Wales, replaced by the **Crown Court** in 1971.

assoilzie

/əˈsɔɪli/

1 In Scots **criminal law**, to acquit or find **not guilty**.

2 In Scots **civil law**, to give **judgment** for the **defender**.

assured shorthold tenancy

A kind of **assured tenancy** which allows the **landlord** to retake possession at the end of a fixed term of at least 6 months without having to give one of the reasons for repossession that would be normal in an assured tenancy. The landlord can get possession at the end of the fixed term by giving at least 2 months' notice (less in some circumstances). **Tenants** can apply to a rent assessment committee, using a form available from law stationers, to set an open market **rent** if they think it is too high.

assured tenancy

The usual kind of tenancy for most new residential lettings made between private landlords and their **tenants** on or after 15 January 1989. The **property** must be let as a separate dwelling and be the tenant's only or main home. There need not be a written agreement. An assured tenancy gives a measure of **security of tenure** at an open market **rent**, agreed between the landlord and tenant but not registered. If the landlord wishes to raise the rent, he or she must give notice and the tenant can apply to a rent assessment committee to set it at open market value. The landlord can regain possession for any of 16 reasons laid down in the Housing Act 1988. These include:

1 non-payment of rent;

2 the landlord's desire to live in the property again having previously lived there;

3 if the property is subject to a mortgage, the landlord's wish to repossess because the lender wants to sell the property to pay off arrears.

The tenant would have to be informed of the possibility of reasons 2 and 3 before the tenancy began.

Three types of assured tenancy differ according to the period for which they run:

1 *Fixed term tenancy*: for a set length of time.

2 *Contractual periodic tenancy*: for an indefinite period, the rent being paid on a weekly or monthly basis.

3 *Statutory periodic tenancy*: automatically created if the tenancy begins as fixed term but at the end of the term the landlord and tenant do not agree to another fixed term or to a contractual periodic tenancy.

A tenant's **marriage** partner or co-habitee has an automatic right to succeed to an assured periodic tenancy if the tenant dies, unless the tenant had already succeeded to the tenancy. The Act gives the right of succession only once.

Partners, or any other combination of people, can negotiate a **joint tenancy** with the landlord. If marriage partners **divorce**, the **court** will decide who gets the tenancy. An unmarried partner who is not a joint tenant will have far fewer rights than a tenant partner.

Under some circumstances, the tenant may assign (pass onto someone else) the tenancy or sub-let it.

attendance centre

A place run by a **local authority** which offenders aged 17–21 may be ordered to attend, for example if a **fine** would be too lenient and a custodial **sentence** too severe.

attorney

A general label for **lawyers** in some countries.

See **power of attorney**.

Attorney-General

The chief legal officer of a nation or state, who represents the government in its legal **actions**. In England and Wales, he or she is an MP and a member of the government. The Scottish counterpart is the **Lord Advocate**. In the USA, the Federal Attorney-General is an appointed member of the President's cabinet.

attour

Scots for *besides* or *over and above*.

automatism

A **defence** to a criminal charge where the **accused** claims his or her conduct was involuntary and unconscious. Examples include **offences** while sleep-walking or in a hypnotic trance. The defence is not available to people who take alcohol or drugs whose effects they know or can reasonably predict.

avizandum

In Scots law, a **judge** *makes avizandum* if he or she considers the **case** privately for a few days.

avoid

To set aside a **voidable contract**.

award

An **arbitrator's judgment**.

B

back-bond
In Scots law, a **deed** or letter qualifying another deed which would otherwise give an absolute right to a **conveyance**.

bail
The release of someone held in legal **custody** pending trial or **appeal** against a **criminal** conviction. Someone granted bail must usually put up a sum of money (*bail in one's own recognizance*) which is forfeit if he or she fails to appear for the trial. A **court** may also require **guarantors** (sureties) to put forward sums of money for the same reason. In a **magistrates' court**, bail should normally be granted unless the court thinks the accused will not turn up for the trial, or will interfere with **witnesses**, or will commit **offences** if let out, or needs to be in custody for self-protection. Serious charges usually preclude bail. Police objections to bail are rarely ignored. An **accused** can appeal against refusal of bail to the **High Court**. About 40% of those acquitted or receiving non-custodial **sentences** spend time in custody beforehand.

Courts may attach special conditions to bail, such as a curfew. A jogger who wore running shorts and exposed himself was forbidden to go jogging in public or to wear shorts; poll tax protestors who had fly-posted were forbidden to handle paper and glue; and a man who regularly went berserk after eating vindaloo was banned from visiting curry houses. In Scotland, monetary bail is unusual; conditions are normally imposed instead.

bailiff
Usually an officer of a **county court** employed to serve **writs**, recover **fines**, **rent** arrears, hire-purchase debts, national insurance contributions etc under procedures dating back to the 12th century. *County court bailiffs* are civil servants, accountable to **judges**. *Private certificated bailiffs* operate under

much less control, though they can be struck off for misconduct. The county court makes a superficial check of their character and references and requires a **bond** to be deposited as surety of good conduct.

Bailiffs seizing goods in settlement of a debt should check that the owner of the goods is the owner of the debt, though they often don't.

Bailiffs may not break down the locked front door of your home unless they are looking for goods belonging to someone else which you are hiding. Once inside, bailiffs may break open an inner door. If you throw the bailiffs out, having first let them in, they can force their way back in, breaking down the front door if necessary. They can also walk into your unlocked home. If they lawfully seize goods, do not lock them in—they can forcibly break out again. In Scotland, similar powers are exercised by sheriff officers (**sheriff court** actions) and Messengers-at-Arms (**Court of Session** and High Court cases).

bailment

In England and Wales, an owner's temporary transfer of possession of goods to another **person**. This includes hiring, loan, and delivery of goods for repair.

See **lien**.

balance of convenience

When a **court** is considering whether to grant an **injunction** or order in a **civil case**, it will judge which side's interests will be more damaged by it. This is the balance of convenience between the two **parties**. The side which will be more damaged is more likely to win this stage of the **action**. For example, in a **case** about whether a newspaper may publish confidential information about a business, the court would judge the business's commercial interests against the value of the **defendant's** right to free speech. As **judges** tend to value property rights very highly, the balance of convenience would be in the business's favour.

bankruptcy

The state of being reduced to financial ruin. Legally, individuals and **partnerships** are in this state when a **court** in bankruptcy proceedings declares them to be bankrupt by a bankruptcy order. These proceedings are started by a **creditor** (or sometimes the **debtor**) presenting a bankruptcy **petition**. It then becomes an **offence** for the debtor to obtain credit of more than £50 without informing the new creditor that he or she is bankrupt. The assets of a bankrupt are held by a **trustee in bankruptcy**. The analogous concept for **limited liability companies** is **insolvency**. In Scotland, similar rules apply.

See **discharge order; public examination; sequestration; undischarged bankrupt**.

bar

1 A legal barrier such as the right not to be tried twice for the same **offence**.

2 An imaginary barrier in a law **court** which protects the **judge** or **magistrate** from being approached except by **barristers, advocates,** court officers and **litigants** in person.

Bar

Barristers or **advocates** as a professional group.

barrister ('counsel')

Someone who passes the profession's examinations and undergoes a vocational training course at the Inns of Court School of Law. This training is usually followed by a year's pupillage in a barrister's **chambers**, six months of which is usually unpaid. Barristers' training and experience are designed to make them more capable of speaking in **court** on a **client's** behalf. Barristers may not form themselves into **limited liability companies**.

No one may qualify as a barrister without eating a certain number of dinners in his or her Inn; this is known as *keeping term*. The Middle Temple requires the consumption of 24—expensive for those living outside London.

Solicitors regularly use barristers to produce a learned **opinion** on the strength of a client's **case** (*counsel's opinion*)—indeed, **legal aid** is often restricted initially to the cost of obtaining such an opinion—or on finer points of law. Clients are not generally supposed to deal directly with barristers, though they can meet and discuss things with them with a solicitor present.

In **court,** barristers wear a wig and the black gown of mourning into which they were put when Queen Anne died in 1714. Nowadays this is said to emphasize the anonymity of the barrister.

Barristers who botch a case in court, perhaps by failing to use a vital piece of **evidence** or calling an important **witness,** cannot be sued for **negligence**. They can, however, be sued for some of their other work, such as a negligent written opinion.

Many clients have been surprised at the sudden appearance of a stand-in barrister just as their case is about to start—their first-choice, who may understand their case intimately, will have been called away on more urgent business. This is especially likely to occur to legally aided clients since the fees are lower. It happens because **barristers' clerks** double-book their barristers, expecting a case to finish on a particular day. Barristers' clerks, however, blame the way that court administrators juggle the listing of cases for trial at short notice.

Few barristers reveal their charges. In London, £150 an hour for advising and drafting, £1,000 a day for appearing in court are fairly common.

Barristers are either *junior counsel* or selected by the Lord Chancellor to be **Queen's** or **King's Counsel**—often called **silks** because their gowns are made of silk. Junior counsel, who wear gowns made of stuff, are not necessarily less competent.

About 85% of the 6,200 barristers in England and Wales are men.

Not all barristers practise law; many use their qualification to work in industry, education etc.

See **cab-rank rule**.

barristers' clerk

The business manager of a group of barristers who acts rather like a theatrical agent, setting and collecting fees and regulating the flow of work. He or she is not usually legally qualified but has wide experience of **courts** and **cases**. The Scottish equivalent is the *advocates' clerk.*

bastard

See **illegitimate**.

battered child

A **child** suffering physical violence at the hands of someone with whom he or she is living. Anyone looking after and living with the child may seek to protect it by an **injunction** under the Domestic Violence and Matrimonial Proceedings Act 1976. A married parent living with the child can use a similar **magistrates' court** proceeding. Similar rules apply in Scotland.

battered wife

A woman suffering physical violence at the hands of her husband. Formerly the police and **courts** were reluctant to become involved in such cases. Now various protections are available from the courts to wives who are also seeking a **divorce**:

1 *a non-molestation order*—this tells the husband not to molest, annoy or behave violently towards her;

2 *an exclusion order*—this keeps him out of the **matrimonial home** for a time, even if he owns it. A power of **arrest** can be attached to the order, whereby the police can arrest the husband if they have reasonable suspicion of his misbehaviour towards his wife.

A wife may also be able to get a *personal protection order* if her husband has already used or threatened violence.

A woman can get some help in the **county court** even if she does not seek divorce or is not married to the batterer:

1 a non-molestation order;

2 an exclusion order, to which a power of arrest can be attached.

Similar rules apply in Scotland.

battery

In England and Wales, the intentional use of force against someone without their consent. It must involve physical contact (unlike **assault**) but not necessarily physical damage. Consent to battery may sometimes be implied, such as during lawful sporting activity. In Scotland, the term *assault* is used.

beg leave

To ask the **court's** permission. Often prefaced, in the mouths of particularly abject **lawyers**, by *humbly*.

See **crave**.

bench

The place where the **judge** or **magistrate** sits in **court**; also, a collective name for a group of judges or magistrates.

beneficiary

See **trust**.

bestiality (zoophilia)

Sexual intercourse with an animal; a **crime**, in certain circumstances, under the Sexual Offences Act 1956. Leading authorities on the subject say it should cease to be a crime except for prosecuting as cruelty any harm done to the animals. Farmers whose sheep, say, are interfered with, might have a **civil action** for trespass on their **property.**

Until 1861 in England and Wales offenders could expect to be executed, in accordance with the strictures of Leviticus. Well into the 1700s the animal would also be put on trial. Nowadays, transgressors can expect short jail terms or suspended **sentences.** In Scotland, the crime is dealt with under **common law.**

bigamy

The **offence** of 'marrying' when already married to someone else. In some countries it is a **defence** to a charge of bigamy if the **accused** has for a period of seven years not known that his or her **marriage** partner was alive. The **prosecution** must prove that the accused knew the partner was alive during that time. Even if the accused is found **not guilty**, the bigamous marriage remains **void**.

bind over

See **breach of the peace; keeping the peace**.

binding in honour only

A phrase used in agreements to show that the **parties** accept that they are not making a legally enforceable **contract**. Football pools coupons (and the rules associated with them) usually include such phrases. 'Winners' who don't get their payout cannot claim, since the coupon is not a contract.

bissextile

In old documents, a leap year, since the sixth day before the start of March used to be reckoned twice, ie on 24th and 25th February. Oblivion would seem an unhappy fate for such a striking word.

blackmail

The **offence** of making an unwarranted demand with menaces. The demand must be made with a view to either personal gain or loss to someone else. The demand is unwarranted unless the **accused** believes he or she has reasonable grounds for it, and that the menaces are appropriate to reinforce the demand. In Scotland and the USA, the term *extortion* is used.

blasphemy

Denying in some scandalous or offensive manner the truth of the Christian religion, the Bible, the Book of Common Prayer, or the existence of God. **Prosecution** is rare. The only successful prosecution in recent times was private—that of Gay News for publishing a salacious poem about Christ. Attempts by Muslims to prosecute Salman Rushdie for writing his 'Satanic Verses' failed since only the Christian God is protected by British blasphemy **laws.**

bodily harm

A criminal **offence** of two types: *grievous bodily harm* (GBH), involving serious physical injury; and *actual bodily harm* (ABH), involving a less serious attack. If someone attempts to commit grievous bodily harm but kills the victim, he or she is **guilty** of **murder.**

bona fide

[Latin: in good faith] Genuine; undertaken in good faith. As in *only bona fide residents are entitled to parking contracts.* The plural, *bona fides,* is often used to mean *credentials.*

bond

In Scots law, a written obligation to pay money or to do some act.

bond and disposition in security

In Scots law, a **mortgage** secured on **heritable property**.

breach of the peace

1 In England and Wales, a disturbance of the public peace, involving harm to people or **property** or fear of **assault.** It is not classed as a **crime. Magistrates** tend to deal with it by binding over miscreants to keep the peace and can impose imprisonment if they refuse to be bound over.

2 In Scotland, a disturbance of the public peace which might reasonably lead to the public being alarmed. This is classed as a crime.

breathalyser

A device used by a uniformed police officer to measure the amount of alcohol in a driver's breath. The driver must be under suspicion of having drunk alcohol above the legal limit, have been involved in an accident, or have committed a traffic **offence** while the car was moving. The driver blows into a tube; crystals in the device change colour if alcohol is present, the extent of the change indicating whether the driver has exceeded the limit (in the UK, 80 mg per litre of blood). If the test is positive, the driver may be arrested and asked to give a specimen of blood, urine or breath at a police station with a doctor present.

Refusal to take the breathalyser or, if positive, one of the other tests without reasonable excuse such as a medical reason, can lead to a **fine,** licence endorsement and disqualification from driving. The same penalties are available on conviction of being over the legal limit for alcohol consumption. The limits are: 80 milligrams (mg) of alcohol in 100 millilitres (ml) of blood; 107 mg of alcohol in 100 ml of urine; and 35 micrograms of alcohol in 100 ml of breath. Depending on the individual's tolerance of alcohol, amount of food eaten and period of consumption, these limits are reached by widely differing levels of consumption.

bribery

The **offence** of deliberately using improper influence on public officials in order to win an advantage. It might involve offering a reward or payment to an official to show favour in the award of a **contract**. An official may not receive or seek such a payment.

brief

A document written by a **solicitor** which explains a **case** to a **barrister** and seeks advice or says what needs to be done. If the brief is from a private **client,** it will be bound in red tape; if from the Crown, white tape.

British Isles

England, Scotland, Wales, Ireland, the Isle of Man, Orkney, the Shetland Islands, the Channel Islands belonging to Great Britain and the islands adjacent to all these.

BS 5750

A standard set by the British Standards Institution concerning quality of administration, eg speed of response to **clients'** letters and phone calls. Solicitors (and other firms) who reach the standard may display the BSI Kite Mark at their premises. The standard does not apply to quality of advice etc.

buggery

Anal intercourse by a man with another man or a woman, or **bestiality** by a man or woman. Buggery (*sodomy* in Scotland) is not a **crime** between consenting males over the age of 21. It is unclear whether it is a crime when a consenting adult woman is involved. Buggery in the armed forces is covered by rules regarding *disgraceful conduct.*

See **homosexuality**.

burden of proof

The duty of a **litigant** or **prosecutor** to prove a **fact**.

See **civil case**.

burglary

In England and Wales, the **crime** of entering a building as a trespasser with the intention of committing **theft,** grievous bodily harm or **rape**; or, having entered, stealing or attempting to steal, or committing or attempting to commit grievous bodily harm. *Building* includes caravans, houseboats and other roofed structures of some permanence.

business name

The name, other than an individual's own, under which a sole trader (or **partnership** or company) does business. The correct names of the owners must be shown on business documents and on business premises. A new business should avoid choosing a name which could lead to confusion with another in the same field or locality, otherwise it runs the risk of being sued for **passing off**.

byelaw (by-law)

A form of **delegated legislation** made by, for example, a local authority or the National Trust. Byelaws concern the regulation, management or administration of a district. Most local authorities have a byelaw concerning *good rule and* *government* which covers street-selling, the playing of loud music in public, spitting in the streets etc. Byelaws may be challenged in the **courts** on the grounds that they are oppressive, uncertain in meaning, contrary to some rule of law, or **ultra vires**.

C

cab-rank rule

A rule among **barristers** that compels them to take any **case** they are offered as long as it is in their usual sphere of work, they are not otherwise engaged, and a proper fee is offered. It is designed to ensure that anyone, no matter how apparently repulsive, has someone to champion their cause. Barristers who wish to get around the rule declare themselves available only for certain kinds of work, such as **administrative law**. A similar rule applies among Scottish **advocates**.

capital punishment

In the UK, death by hanging. The **penalty** was abolished for **murder** in 1965; the last execution occurred at Preston in 1964. In civilian life the penalty remains mandatory for **treason** and for piracy when murder is attempted, though the sovereign may exercise clemency. Under military **law** the death penalty is theoretically available for various **offences** including serious misconduct in action, mutiny or incitement to mutiny, communicating with the enemy and obstructing operations. Subjects of some former British colonies, such as Jamaica, have the right to **appeal** against the death sentence to the British Privy Council.

Attempts to restore capital punishment have repeatedly failed in Parliament. Several notorious **miscarriages of justice** in the 1980s, where the 'offenders' would probably have been executed had the penalty been available, have lessened the likelihood of the death penalty's reintroduction for murder.

car boot sale

An event where private individuals sell goods, usually of low value, from their car boot or a small stall. Such sales are not covered by the consumer protection that applies to the customers of traders.

careless driving

The **offence,** carrying a maximum fine of £1,000, of driving a vehicle on a road without due care and attention. It usually relates to errors of judgment rather than **negligence** and carries 3–9 penalty points under **totting-up.** There is a similar offence for cyclists.

care order

See **children in care.**

case

A proceeding in **civil** or **criminal law,** or something that forms sufficient grounds for bringing an action in civil law.

case law

Law based on **judges'** decisions in **cases,** rather than the written law enacted by **Parliament.**
See **common law; precedent.**

case stated

A type of **appeal.** An appeal is said to be *by case stated* if it claims not that the **facts** found were wrong, but that the **court's** decision relating to the facts was wrong in **law** or outside the court's powers. It is a common form of appeal against conviction in the **magistrates' court.** In Scotland the usual equivalent is *stated case.*

casus belli

[Latin: case for war] In **international law,** an event justifying or providing an excuse for war.

Category A prisoner

A prisoner in the highest security category reserved for the most dangerous offenders or suspects or those whose escape would be most embarrassing to the **Home Office.**

causation

The relationship between an action and its consequences. A prosecutor must usually prove that some action of the **accused** brought about the result for which he or she stands trial, and that the accused intended the result or was **reckless** about whether it occurred.

In a **civil case**, the **plaintiff** must prove that the **defendant's** actions or lack of them caused the injury, damage or loss complained of; without this causal link, the plaintiff gets nothing. However, the court decides this on the balance of probabilities—in other words, was there at least a 51% chance that the defendant's actions caused the injury? If so, the plaintiff will win. Causation, said Lord Reid in a judgment in 1953, must be determined by applying common sense to the **facts** of each particular **case**.

See **proximate cause**.

Cause List

A **court's** printed list of **cases** for the day, displayed on a notice board. The Scottish equivalent is the *Rolls of Court*.

cause of action

The **facts** or allegations which enable someone to **sue**.

causing death by reckless driving

The **offence** of reckless driving which unintentionally results in death. The **sentence** is up to 5 years in prison or a **fine** or both, compulsory disqualification for at least 2 years, and 4 penalty points under **totting-up**. In a case in 1981, Lord Diplock spoke of reckless driving as 'driving in such a manner as to create an obvious and serious risk of causing physical injury to some other road user and doing so without having given any thought to the possibility of there being any such risk or, having recognized that there was some risk involved, nonetheless going on to take it.'

caution

1 A warning from a police officer: 'You do not have to say anything unless you wish to do so, but what you say may be given in **evidence**.' This must be said before any questions are put to someone suspected of a **crime**. The caution does not

mean that the suspect will be charged with the **offence**. If the suspect is not under **arrest,** the officer must say so and, if the caution is given at a police station, tell the suspect that he or she is free to leave, and mention that the suspect can take legal advice.

2 A warning from a police officer, on releasing a suspect without charge, that if he or she is reported for another offence, the circumstances of the first alleged offence may be taken into account.

3 In Scots law, where caution is pronounced to rhyme with *nation,* it is a security which people carrying out some kinds of duty (such as the administrator of a **will**) must obtain as a safeguard in case they mishandle the money. Insurers will put up a *bond of caution* in return for a premium. *Cautioner* corresponds to the English **guarantor.**

caveat

[Latin: beware] A notice entered in a register to warn people that they must not do something without first informing the **person** who makes the caveat. Someone who claims an interest in a dead person's **estate** might enter a caveat with the Probate Registry, ensuring that his or her **claim** will be dealt with when the estate is distributed.

caveat emptor

[Latin: Let the buyer beware] A maxim which warns buyers that they cannot claim from the seller if the purchase is defective. Traders' rights to rely on this principle have been modified by consumer law, notably by the Sale of Goods Act 1979 which says that the goods must be fit for the purpose for which they are sold and of **merchantable quality**. In sales of land, sellers must ensure that they are indeed the true owners and have the right to sell it, and that it is free from **encumbrances** that the buyer was unaware of.

See **fit for purpose; satisfactory quality**.

cedent

In Scots law, one who contractually assigns a right to a **third party**, known as the *assignee.*

Central Criminal Court

The Old Bailey, the **Crown Court** for Central London, built on the site of the former Newgate prison. There are 19 courts in it. Its dome is topped by a statue of a woman holding the scales of **justice**; despite popular belief, she does not wear a blindfold.

certiorari

See **judicial review**.

chambers

1 The **judge's** room or private office behind the **court**. When **hearings** are held in chambers, **barristers** do not wear their wigs and robes.

2 The offices of a barrister or group of barristers.

chancellor

In Scots law, a **jury** foreman.

change of name

Someone may change surname by using a different name so consistently that he or she becomes generally known by it. The surname may also be changed by newspaper advertisement, *statutory declaration* or, in England and Wales, by **deed** poll.

Making a statutory declaration is cheap, and effective for most purposes though some foreign countries only recognize a name changed by deed poll. Simply write or type a suitable form of words and take it to a **solicitor** or **commissioner for oaths** who will ask you to authenticate it by swearing an **oath**. There will be a fee of about £5. A suitable form of words might be: 'I, Joan Kelvin, of (address) do solemnly declare that I was formerly known as Joan King but that I have adopted and wish from now on to use the surname of Kelvin. I make this declaration conscientiously, believing it to be true, under the Statutory Declarations Act 1835: signed Joan Kelvin, formerly King.'

A parent cannot change a **child's** surname without the other parent's consent.

character
See **sentence**.

charge
1 A criminal accusation against someone, usually by the police.

2 In Scots law, a **judge** *charges the jury* by telling them what they must consider to reach a **verdict**. It can also mean an order to obey a court **decree**. A charge is a prerequisite of a **poinding**, being a requirement to the debtor to pay or perform an obligation within a given time.

charge on land
An **interest** in **land**, such as a **mortgage**. It secures a loan by giving the **creditor** the right to money from the income or sale of the land, in preference to **unsecured creditors**.

chattel
An item of personal **moveable property** such as jewellery or an **interest** in **land** less than a **freehold** interest.

child
1 Usually a child who has not reached 14, but different UK **laws** give different definitions.

2 An offspring of parents. In **wills** etc, child is taken to include a child born outside the **marriage** and an adopted child of the marriage.

child abuse
Molesting of **children** by parents or others who have **parental responsibility**. If it is of a sexual nature, the **offence** may be **indecent assault** or **gross indecency**.

child assessment order
If a local authority in England and Wales has **reasonable** cause to suspect that a **child** is suffering significant harm (perhaps from its parents) it can ask the **court** to make such an order. The assessment which follows will help the local authority decide what steps to take next.

See **emergency protection order**.

child of the family

A **child** under 18 whom the **law** regards as a couple's child even though it is not born to or adopted by them, on the grounds that they have treated it as their own.

Child Care Panel

In England and Wales, a specialist panel of **solicitors** set up by the Law Society to represent **children** in care proceedings. A list of Panel members is available in citizens advice bureaux and **magistrates' courts.**

children in care

In England and Wales, **children** taken into the care of a **local authority** which assumes many or all of the parents' rights and responsibilities. Parents can demand the child's return at any time, though the **local authority** may apply to the **court** for a court order if it is concerned for the child's welfare.

For a child to be taken into care, a court must impose a **care order,** often following an application from a local authority or the NSPCC. An order can only be made if the child is suffering or is likely to suffer significant harm because of a lack of **reasonable** parental care or because it is beyond parental control. The harm the child suffers must be significant, so minor shortcomings affecting health and development should not give rise to intervention. Parents need not be at fault before a care order can be made; they may simply be unable to adequately care for the child or the child may be beyond their control. Parents can **appeal** against the order. Normally local authorities must allow children in care to have a reasonable amount of contact with their parents or **guardians**. Similar rules apply in Scotland.

chose

A thing. It may be a *chose in possession* (a physical thing like a jewel or book), or a *chose in action* (a right that can be enforced by legal action).

circuit judge

In England and Wales, judges who, in the **Crown Court**, deal with serious **criminal** cases (but rarely **murder**) and, in the **county court**, deal with minor **civil cases**. They tend to be competent senior **barristers** who have decided they can go no further at the **Bar** and opt for the security and pension of a minor judgeship. They are referred to as *His (or Her) Honour Judge Surname QC* (if a QC). In court they are addressed as *Your honour, Sir, Madam* or, at the Old Bailey, *My Lord*. They are paid £50,000 a year, less than they would expect as barristers, and retire at 72.

Circuit judges, unlike **High Court** judges, do not go on **circuit**. The name is a relic of the days (from 1100 onwards) when they travelled the country dispensing the royal **justice**.

circuit

One of the regions of England and Wales into which court administration is divided.

circumcision, female

The cutting off or mutilating of a woman's external genitals. This is an **offence** punishable by up to 5 years in prison; it is also an offence to help a woman mutilate herself in this way. In Scotland the offence is covered by **assault**.

circumstantial evidence (indirect evidence)

Evidence of circumstances from which a **judge** or **jury** may presume the existence of a **fact** without direct **proof**.

See **direct evidence**.

citizen's arrest

An **arrest** by someone who is not a police officer. Anyone may arrest an individual who has committed or is committing an arrestable offence, or whom they reasonably suspect of doing so. They may use **reasonable force**. Someone wrongfully arrested may **sue** the performer of the arrest for false imprisonment.

Citizen's Charter

British government proposals in 1991 which, if implemented, would enable citizens to demand certain standards of service from government agencies and **local authorities**. Legal rights given by the charter would enable citizens to more easily win **compensation** if, for example, they were inconvenienced by a strike (or threat of a strike) by railway employees or public sector workers. The proposals would not require **litigants** to prove actual loss—a major extension of their present rights to claim **damages** under **civil** law.

civil case

[Latin *civis*: a citizen] A legal **action** between private interests. For example, a **person** may **sue** another for some harm caused to him or her, for breach of **contract**, or for money owed. The police are not involved unless the same behaviour amounts to a **crime**. Drivers convicted of the crime of **reckless driving** might be sued in the **civil courts** for **negligence** by the people they injured. A murderer could be sued by the victim's close relatives.

Civil cases are decided on the balance of probabilities (ie, is the **plaintiff's** story more likely than not to be true?). This is a much lower **standard of proof** than in criminal cases. Civil cases are governed by **civil law**, also known as *private law*.

See **criminal law**.

civil court

A court that hears civil rather than criminal **cases**. In England the main civil courts are the **county courts** and the **High Court**. In Scotland, the main civil courts are the **Sheriff Court** and the **Court of Session**.

civil law

See **civil case**; **civil wrong**.

civil wrong

An infringement of someone's rights for which they can sue for **damages** or some other **remedy**. Lawyers call it **tort** in England and **delict** in Scotland

claim

A demand for a **court** to put right an alleged wrong, or the assertion of a right.

See **pleadings; statement of claim**.

Clarity

An organization, mainly of **lawyers,** which seeks to clarify written and spoken legal language so that people affected by legal documents and **court** proceedings can more easily understand them. Clarity's newsletter remarks: 'Customary legal language is a mess, but the misuse of language is the result of a want of skill, not the wickedness of 50 000 conspiring individuals [**solicitors**].'

class action

A legal **action** in which individuals who claim to have been cheated or injured by a business or government body can club together and **sue** for **compensation**. The aim is to simplify and shorten the process of obtaining **justice,** and stop individuals being picked off one by one by a wealthy **defendant**.

In Britain class actions are rare, but in 1991 3 500 people began suing 9 different manufacturers of tranquillizers for their alleged addictive effects. The case involves 300 **solicitors'** firms. Their work is being co-ordinated by a nucleus of 6 firms to avoid duplicating the research.

clean hands

A phrase from one of the maxims which underpin **equity,** a body of legal principles: *he who comes to equity must come with clean hands.* In other words, someone who makes a **claim** in equity must have behaved properly over the subject matter of the claim.

Clerk of Justiciary

In Scotland, the principal clerk of the High Court of Justiciary.

Clerk of Session

In Scotland, the principal clerk of the **Court of Session**.

clerk of the court
See **magistrates' court**.

client
A **person** who engages a **solicitor**. Also, when a solicitor instructs a **barrister**, the solicitor is the barrister's client.

closed record
In Scots law, a written **statement** of the **case** on which the **parties** seek the **court's** decision. In *record*, the stress is on the second syllable.

code of practice
A body of rules which lack legal force but give practical guidance, like the Highway Code. Breach of a code of practice does not expose someone to **prosecution** or a **civil** claim, but it can be used as **evidence** that a **law** has been broken.

codicil
A **schedule** or supplement to a **will** which the maker of the will uses to add, explain, alter or retract something in the will.

cognition
In Scots law, a rare judicial process by which someone might be found insane.

cognizant
Aware of, pompously. The citation in an award for exports says: *We being cognizant of the outstanding achievement of the said body as manifested in the furtherance and increase of the Export Trade of our United Kingdom . . . and being desirous of showing Our Royal Favour do hereby confer upon it The Queen's Award for Export Achievement.* Some **lawyer,** somewhere, must believe that the monarch speaks like this.

cohabitation
Living together as husband and wife, whether or not legally married. Someone in such an arrangement is a co-habitee.

See **cohabitation contract; common law wife; pre-marital contracts**.

cohabitation contract

A **contract** which sets out the rights and obligations of a man and a woman who live together outside **marriage**. The contract might cover property rights, child care responsibilities etc. Such contracts have not been tested in the **courts,** so they are still not widely used. The Scottish Law Commission has recommended that **Parliament** should legislate to give such contracts clear legal status. It is probable that a court would at least uphold any contract provisions regarding **property**. Many **lawyers** believe that if two adults freely agree to live together under certain terms, the **law** should give effect to that agreement. Others believe that a court should not regard a social and domestic arrangement as legally binding.

See **common law marriage; pre-marital contracts**.

cohabitation rule

A social security rule under which the resources and requirements of an unmarried couple living together are totalled when their right to benefits is assessed.

collateral

Security that is separate and additional to the main security for a debt. In Scots **law** concerning rights of succession, the terms means, strictly, brothers and sisters.

commissioner for oaths

Someone appointed by the **Lord Chancellor** to administer **oaths** or take **affidavits**. Practising **solicitors** are commissioners for oaths. They must not use their powers as commissioners in **cases** in which they are acting or have an **interest**.

Commission of the European Communities

The administration of the **European Communities** (EC). Its powers include presenting proposals for EC **law** to the Council, making law where the Council permits it to, administering EC law (eg granting import and export licences, raising levies, paying subsidies), taking decisions and issuing opinions on breaches of EC law, imposing fines for breaches of EC law, prohibiting anti-competitive practices, and prosecuting breaches of EC law by member states before the **European Court of Justice.**

commit for trial

To refer a **case** from a **magistrates' court** to the **Crown Court** for trial.

committal in civil proceedings

A method of enforcing a **court judgment** by obtaining a court order that someone be committed to prison. Commonly the order is used when the individual has committed **contempt of court,** but it can be used to enforce an order for payment of a debt.

committal proceedings

A **hearing** in a **magistrates' court** concerning an **offence** which is too serious for summary trial. The **bench** acts as an examining magistrate and may commit the **accused** for trial. Usually, severe reporting restrictions are in place. There are two types of **committal proceeding:**

1 The **evidence** is not considered in detail nor are **witnesses** examined. The evidence must be presented in writing, the accused must have a **solicitor** acting for him or her in the **case,** and the solicitor must not wish to say that there is no case to answer. The **defence** can require a full examination of the **facts** to be heard.

2 The evidence is produced and the accused is asked to make a **statement** but not to plead **guilty** or **not guilty** as this is an assessment of the strength of the case not a trial.

commonhold

The name given to a proposal in 1991 that leaseholders of blocks of flats (in England and Wales) whose original **leases** had 21 or more years to run should be able to purchase their **freehold** and manage the **property** themselves as a group. To be able to purchase, at least two-thirds of these long leaseholders would have to agree, and they must comprise at least two-thirds of all the leaseholders, short and long, in the block.

The freehold price would be based on the price which would be paid between a freeholder willing to sell and an existing leaseholder willing to buy. Certain blocks of flats would not be purchasable in this way, such as those in which the freeholder actually lived.

Obtaining the freehold would avoid owning a property which loses value or even becomes impossible to sell as the lease reduces and eventually reverts to the freehold **landlord** when the lease expires. It would also lessen the problem of landlords who fail to maintain their properties well.

See **leasehold.**

common land

Land registered with **local authorities** as giving the *right of common,* meaning a right of someone to profit from another **person's** land or water in a certain way, for example: *common of pasture*—the right to feed animals on the land; *common of piscary*—the right to fish; *common of turbary*—the right to cut turf; *common of estovers*—the right to take necessary wood for furnishing; and *common in the soil*—the right to dig for minerals etc. There is no common land in Scotland and Northern Ireland.

common law

Law based on rules developed by the royal courts in the three centuries after the Norman Conquest in 1066. Common law is thus rooted in the ancient, unwritten law of England, as distinct from the written or **statute** law. Common law has been developed over the years by the **judges, case** by case, by analogy with earlier cases; hence it is sometimes called **judge-made law.** Most of the law of **contract** and **tort** is common law, so decisions in such cases tend to be based on **precedent. Lawyers** find it useful to remember—or be able to locate— judgments in important old cases and keep abreast of significant new ones.

Some of the roots of the common law are found in the venerated works of five long-dead gentlemen of the law: Bracton, Littleton, Coke, Hale and Blackstone.

Bracton was probably Henry of Bratton, an **assize** judge from 1248 to 1268. He produced a textbook in about 1256 which set out the line of argument and the decision in important cases.

Littleton was a judge from 1466 to 1481. He set down the essentials of medieval land law which helped to maintain the power and influence of feudalism for several centuries.

Coke (pronounced Cook) was Sir Edward Coke (1552–1633) who became Chief Justice of the King's Bench in 1613. He translated Littleton's 'Tenures' into English. This is referred to as Coke upon Littleton (Co. Litt.), a standard textbook on land law for many generations. In many ways Coke made the law, for although some of his propositions lacked any basis in case law or statute, his learning gave them the force of law. Judges seeking guidance would refer to Coke, and still occasionally do.

Hale (1609–76) was Sir Matthew Hale, another Chief Justice whose various books were published after his death without the benefit of his final revisions. His view that a man cannot rape his wife, since she is deemed to have given her consent by **marriage** to **sexual intercourse** in all circumstances, prevailed until 1991.

Blackstone was the 18th century MP and judge Sir William Blackstone whose 'Commentaries' described the workings of the English legal system. Their publication came on the eve of the American Revolution and strongly influenced the development of American law. Compared with most previous legal writers, Blackstone wrote clearly and put simple summaries in the margins.

Among the heroes of the common law in Scotland are Viscount Stair (1619–1695), whose 'Institutions of the Law of Scotland' was published in 1681, and Baron Hume (1757–1838), whose 'Commentaries' on the **criminal law** appeared in 1797.

common law marriage

A **marriage** recognized as valid in **law** even though it does not comply with the usual legal requirements for marriage. Today this applies only in such rare cases as marriages celebrated overseas where no local form of marriage is reasonably available to the **parties,** or some marriages celebrated by military chaplains. Newspaper descriptions of people as *common-law wives* are therefore usually false.

On marriage, a woman acquires such rights as an automatic share of the husband's property and to financial support if the marriage breaks down. (The same rights apply to her husband.) Without marriage, a woman who cohabits with a man may acquire some or all of the same rights in time, but is not certain to do so. If they split up and there is a legal dispute about money and **property**, a **court** would look at the individual **facts** of the **case** in deciding what the parties were entitled to.

See **cohabitation contract**.

community home

A place where **children in care** are looked after under local authority control.

community law

The **law** of the **European Community** (EC). The law consists of the treaties establishing the European Economic Community ('Common Market' or EEC) such as the founding Treaty of Rome, 25 March 1957, and amending treaties such as the Single European Act, 1986, EC legislation (Regulations and Directives), Decisions of the European Commission, and judgments of the Court of Justice of the European Communities and Court of First Instance (European Court). This law forms part of the law of each member state. It overrides national law if there is inconsistency between the two.

The most important European Court decisions are published in the Common Market Law Reports and European Court Reports. The latter are the 'official' reports of the court's decisions.

See **Commission of the European Communities; Court of Human Rights; European Court of Justice; European Parliament; European Community Directive; European Community Regulation**.

community legislation

Provisions of the **European Community** treaties and **law** made by the **Council of Ministers** or the **Commission of the European Communities**, usually after consultation or co-operation with the **European Parliament**. This law affects much (if not yet all) of UK law, including agriculture, the free movement of workers, services and goods, social security, competition and some aspects of company law.

See **community law**.

community service order

If an individual aged 17 or over is convicted of an **offence** punishable with imprisonment, the **court** may require him or her to perform unpaid work for a specified number of hours under a probation officer's supervision—a community service order. Breach of the order can lead to substitution of the punishment that would originally have been imposed.

compearance

In Scots law, the appearing of a **defender** in **court**.

compensation

See **Criminal Injuries Compensation Board**.

compensation order

A **court** order saying that an **offender** (or, in the case of a juvenile, his or her parents) must pay money to compensate the victim of a **crime**.

conclusion

In Scots law, a **statement** in a **summons** of the precise **relief** which the **pursuer** seeks. To claim in this way is to *conclude for.*

condescendence

In Scots law, the part of a **pursuer's pleadings** which state the **facts** on which he or she relies.

condition

An important obligation in a **contract,** one which goes *to the root of the contract.* Breach of a condition gives the innocent party the right to treat the contract as ended. A minor obligation in a contract is a **warranty,** breach of which does not allow the innocent party the right to end the contract, though an **action** for **damages** may succeed.

confession

Admission of guilt by an **accused** which is written down by police and, usually, signed by the accused. Under English **law** it need not be corroborated by other **evidence,** such as identification of the suspect by **witnesses;** in Scotland it must be.

Under the stress of being taken into **custody** some people are known to have confessed to crimes they have not committed. One man, whom the police deprived of access to a solicitor for 7 weeks, confessed to **murder** and was imprisoned for 16 years before being released in 1992 on the basis of evidence which appears to have been withheld from his defence at his trial.

Statistical comparisons between the language of a confession and an accused's normal speech pattern can show whether the accused is likely to have been the author.

confidence, law of

In **civil law**, the **courts** recognize that publication of certain information breaches the duty of confidentiality that may exist between, for example, an employer and employee or a husband and wife. An employee who reveals an employer's secret processes or a nanny who reveals the domestic secrets of the household could be sued for breach of confidence. The courts distinguish, however, between tittle tattle and important secrets. Employers who can foresee that their secrets could be disclosed may extend their rights under civil law by getting employees to sign *confidentiality contracts.* Even so, a common **defence** in such cases is that disclosure was in the public interest. A partner in a highly public **marriage** would be unlikely to persuade the courts that the other partner had breached confidentiality by selling the marriage secrets to a newspaper.

Remedies for breach of confidence are to **sue** for **damages** or get an **injunction** imposing *prior restraint* on publication. Newspapers have sometimes had difficulty getting these prior restraints, known as *interim injunctions*, lifted. An injunction in 1981 stopped Thames Television's scheduled screening of a documentary about the pregnancy drug, Primodos. The programme wished to refer to material which the producer, while working as a consultant for the drug's makers, had seen. Lord Denning argued that the programme should be shown, saying that 'the public interest in receiving information about the drug . . . far outweighs the private interest of the makers in preventing discussion of it.' But he was overruled by less senior **judges** sitting with him, who gave precedence to the firm's rights of confidence even though the information itself, unlike a **trade secret**, was not valuable.

Breach of confidence **cases** have become more common because English law has no specific law against invasion of **privacy**.

confirmation

In Scots law, the **sheriff's** permission to an **executor** of someone's **estate** to wind up the estate. The executor obtains it on **petition** to the sheriff of the area where the individual lived.

consistorial actions

In Scots law, **actions** between husband and wife about **marriage, divorce,** legitimacy of **children,** separation and *putting to silence*—the prevention of someone from maintaining that a child is the legitimate child of someone who says it isn't. These actions are usually dealt with in the **Court of Session**.

conspiracy

The **offence** committed by two or more people who agree that one or some of them will commit a **crime**. The crime is complete once agreement is reached, even though nothing more is done. It is punishable by the same **sentence** as if the crime had been carried out. It is not conspiracy if the only other individual with whom you make such an agreement is your **marriage** partner.

There is also a **tort** of conspiracy; this is committed when a group of people decide to do something unlawful, or to do something lawful using unlawful means, with the aim of causing loss to someone. If that individual's **interests** are harmed, he or she can **sue**. This does not apply to some aspects of **trade disputes** nor to protecting one's own legitimate trade interests.

conspiracy to pervert the course of justice
See **perverting the course of justice**.

constructive dismissal
Resigning your job because the effect of your employer's actions was to make your working conditions so intolerable that you had no choice but to resign. You may be able to **sue** for **wrongful dismissal**.

constructive notice
This means that if you didn't see the **notice,** you are regarded as having done so. Sometimes a legal notice can be given in a press advertisement or a journal like the **London Gazette**. This is taken to be sufficient notice to anyone who may have an **interest**.

contempt of court
1 In **civil law**, disobedience of a **court** order.

2 In **criminal law,** conduct which obstructs the administration of **justice,** such as interfering with **witnesses,** causing a disturbance in court, reporting jury room discussions or publishing material which impedes a fair trial.

Both civil and criminal contempt can be punished by a **fine** or imprisonment.

contra proferentem
[Latin: against the individual putting it forward] A rule of **interpretation** saying that if a phrase in a **contract** is ambiguous, it will be given the interpretation which is less favourable to the **person** relying on the contract. It therefore applies particularly to terms limiting or excluding liability, especially in preprinted standard form contracts.

contract

A legally binding agreement composed of certain essential elements:

1 The contract must arise out of an intention by both **parties** to create a legally enforceable relationship between them.

2 One party must make an **offer** which the other party accepts in identical terms.

3 Unless the contract is made by **deed,** there must be *consideration,* meaning that one side gives some benefit or suffers some loss in return for the promise made. (Consideration might be as little as a penny.)

In addition, the parties must have *legal capacity,* such as being at least 18 or mentally capable. The contract must be lawful— an agreement to commit **murder,** for example, is **void** and neither side would be able to **sue** for the return of any money paid. Some kinds of contract need not be in writing—buying something in a shop creates an unwritten contractual agreement. A contract to buy **land** must be in writing or there must be some evidence of it before anyone could be sued over it.

In Scotland, a contract can be made without consideration, when it is called a *gratuitous contract.*

See **invitation to treat; puff; privity of contract; void contract; voidable contract; wrongful dismissal.**

contributory negligence

If a **court** decides that a **plaintiff** contributed to his or her own injury, it can reduce the **damages** payable by the other side. A plaintiff who was 25% to blame for an accident would have the damages reduced accordingly.

contumacious

A grandiose description of someone a **judge** considers disobedient of the **court.**

conversion

Dealing with goods so as to deny the owner's rights, or claiming rights inconsistent with those of the owner. Conversion is a **tort** which is not recognized in Scotland.

conveyance

A written document (usually a **deed**) which, when signed, sealed and delivered, transfers an **interest** in **land** from one to another. Hence *conveyancing*. (Sealing is not required in Scotland.) On the sale of a house, a conveyance is drawn up so as to transfer ownership of the **property** effectively. In England and Wales, in the case of land which has been registered, a completed form transferring the land must be lodged at the district land registry in order to transfer the legal interest.

Solicitors and **licensed conveyancers** may carry out the work of conveyancing for a fee. Licensed conveyancers are subject to the professional controls of the Council for Licensed Conveyancers. Individuals may perform their own conveyancing, though with certain kinds of work, such as complex leasehold properties, a detailed knowledge of the **law** is an advantage.

See **seal**.

co-obligant

See **joint and several**.

copyright

The right to reproduce or allow others to reproduce original works of art, drama, literature or music. The Copyright Act 1988 also covers radio and television broadcasts and films. Copyright lasts during the author's lifetime and for 50 years afterwards (50 years after the end of the year of transmission in the case of broadcasts and films). Copyright can be sold and given by **will**. The symbol © or the word 'copyright' do not have to be present for the author to have copyright; it exists automatically. The usual **remedies** for breach of copyright include an **action** for **damages** and **injunction**.

co-respondent

Someone with whom a married individual is alleged to have committed adultery. He or she may be asked to give **evidence** during **divorce** proceedings.

coroner

In England and Wales, a public officer who investigates the cause of death, especially if there is suspicion that it was not due to natural causes or if it occurred in prison or police **custody**. The coroner may order a **post mortem** examination or hold an official inquiry, an **inquest**. Coroners must be qualified **lawyers** or doctors. Inquests are not trials, but **witnesses** are called and there is often a **jury** to decide on the manner of death—**suicide**, misadventure, unlawful killing or accident. If they are not sure, they can record an *open verdict*. Coroners also hold inquests on **treasure trove** and can order bodies to be dug up.

corporation

[Latin *corpus*: a body] An organization created by the process of incorporation. This process provides a legal identity—called a legal **person**—separate from the human beings who work for it. In other words, the people come and go, but the corporation lives on until brought to an end by a proper legal process. There are two types:

1 *corporations aggregate*—such as a limited company, usually created by registration with the Registrar of Companies;

2 *corporations sole*—much rarer and created only by **statute**. These are official positions which have a separate legal identity from the man or woman who occupies them, like the monarch or the Archbishop of Canterbury. Their **property** may be used by the holder of the position but does not belong to the holder personally.

See **limited liability company.**

corroboration

In **court** proceedings, **evidence** that confirms other evidence. In Scots law, a **fact** cannot usually be proved by the testimony of one individual alone—there must be other testimony or facts or circumstances which amount to corroboration.

See **confession**.

costs

The expenses of a **court hearing**. The term is also applied to legal fees.

Council of Ministers of the European Communities

The body which generally has the final say on all **European Community law**. It comprises representatives (government ministers) from each of the member states.

council tax

A tax proposed to replace the community charge in 1993. The amount of tax will be based on the **property's** value and the number of adults in the property. The standard bill will be for two adults per household, with a 25% discount for single householders.

counsel

A **barrister** or **advocate**.

counterclaim

Legal **action** by a **defendant** which cuts across the **plaintiff's claim** by making a claim against the plaintiff.

counterfeiting

Imitating some object (chiefly, currency notes and coin) in order to pass off the imitation as genuine. It is an **offence** to counterfeit or alter coin currently in circulation.

county court

A type of **court** in England and Wales concerned with civil disputes. County courts deal mainly with **contract** and **tort** cases, **landlord** and **tenant** disputes, matrimonial cases including undefended **divorce,** and the **small claims** procedure. The county court ranks lower in the hierarchy of courts than the **High Court**.

See **small claims**.

court

A place where the justice system decides legal cases. It often consists of courtrooms, judges' rooms, barristers' robing rooms, a library and administration offices, canteens, and public seating and public waiting areas.

There has been pressure to improve court facilities for the benefit of members of the public who attend, such as **witnesses** and friends of the **accused**. Criticism has focused on lack of seating, poor or non-existent canteens and toilets, lack of private areas for **clients** to discuss their cases without being overheard by eavesdroppers and their opponents, and the lack of separation of **prosecution** witnesses from the friends of the accused—a considerable ordeal, for example, for an **assault** victim.

The listing of **cases** also causes concern, with perhaps 30 cases being listed to be heard at one time. Not only does this waste the time of **litigants,** witnesses and **solicitors,** it appears to substantiate the view that courts are run primarily to suit **judges,** not the public. But one advantage of listing so many cases for simultaneous **hearing** is that it encourages **out-of-court settlements.**

See **county court; Court of Appeal; Court of Human Rights; Court of Session; Crown Court; magistrates' court.**

court artist

Someone employed by a newspaper or television company to sketch courtroom scenes from memory for publication. Drawing and photography are not allowed in the courtroom, so artists make notes about their subjects.

court martial

A **court** which tries **offences** against armed services law, such as mutiny or desertion. The court comprises serving officers who sit without a **jury** and are advised on the law by a judge advocate, a **barrister.** Convictions and **sentences** are subject to confirmation by higher military authority. Convictions can be appealed against to the Courts-Martial Appeal Court, consisting of the **Lord Chief Justice** and other members of the

Supreme Court, and ultimately to the **House of Lords.** Serious offences under the **criminal law** are likely to be tried in the ordinary criminal courts.

The plural is *courts martial,* as martial is adjectival.

Court of Appeal

An English **court** with civil and criminal divisions which hears **appeals** from other courts. The civil division hears appeals from the **High Court** and the **county court**; its head is the **Master of the Rolls.** The criminal division hears appeals from the **Crown Court;** its head is the **Lord Chief Justice.** Appeal on a point of **law** may be allowed from the Court of Appeal to the **House of Lords.**

court of first instance

The **court** where the first decision on a **case** is made, as opposed to a court where an **appeal** is heard.

Court of Human Rights

A **court** in Strasbourg, France, set up by the **European Convention of Human Rights** which Britain has signed. It acts as a court of last resort for victims of breaches of the convention. It has made several rulings against the British Government on the rights of prisoners, mental patients, immigrants, and the right not to be caned in schools. The court can only be approached through the European Commission on Human Rights which the convention also set up. The commission can only investigate a complaint if the applicant has tried all possible **remedies** in the national courts including, in England, the **House of Lords.** The commission will try to reach a friendly settlement between the **parties.** If this fails, the **case** may finally reach the Court of Human Rights. Only a handful of cases are dealt with every year.

Court of Session

The Superior Scottish Civil Court which sits only in Edinburgh. It has an **Outer House** and a more senior **Inner House**, analogous to the English **High Court** and **Court of Appeal** respectively.

court order

An order given by a **court,** often in the form of a document to which the court **seal** is attached. Disobedience of a court order may be **contempt of court.**

covenant

1 [Noun] A written document under **seal** (not in Scotland), also known as a **deed.** It contains a promise to act in a certain way. In some cases there may be a tax advantage. Members of charities covenant their subscriptions, enabling the charity to reclaim from the **Inland Revenue** a sum equal to the tax paid.

Covenants do not have to be full of **saids, aforesaids** and other legal mumbo-jumbo, though they often are; a **lawyer** should be able to draft one in everyday English. Charities will often supply a suitable form of words.

2 [Verb] To agree by signing a **deed.**

covenant to repair

A clause in most **leases** showing each side's obligations to make repairs.

crave

To make a formal request to a **court;** part of the bootlicking language which some **lawyers** believe impresses **judges.** In Scotland, the word is also used as a noun for part of the **Sheriff Court's** initial **writ.**

creditor

Someone to whom money is owed by a **debtor.**

crime

See **actus reus; mens rea; offence.**

Criminal Injuries Compensation Board

The public body which awards money to victims of **crime** or accidental injury occurring while taking an exceptional risk in the prevention of crime.

Victims must normally **claim** within 3 years of the incident and must normally report it promptly to the police. The minimum **compensation** is £750, so the Board disregards minor injuries. The Board takes into account the victim's conduct at the time of the incident—did he or she contribute to its cause?—and his or her criminal record, if any. A victim who continues to live with the offender cannot succeed in a claim; the offender must not be seen to benefit.

Victims who are claiming state benefits because of low income may find that an **award** takes them over the savings limit for receiving benefits and reductions in community charge.

criminal law

[Latin *crimen*: a crime, verdict or accusation] A branch of **law** which deals with **offences** against society generally. Investigation is usually a police responsibility. In England and Wales, responsibility for **prosecution** rests with the **Crown Prosecution Service**; in Scotland, with the **procurator fiscal**. **Private prosecutions** are possible but rare. In a criminal case, the prosecution must show beyond all reasonable doubt that the **accused** is **guilty**—a higher **standard of proof** than required in a **civil case**.

criminal trespass

See **trespassers will be prosecuted**.

cross-examination

The questioning in **court** of a **witness** called by the other side.

Crown Court

A **court** in England and Wales which deals with serious **crimes** such as **murder, rape, arson** and **fraud,** as well as less serious **offences. Theft** involving a few pounds can go to the **Crown Court** if the **accused** pleads **not guilty** in the **magistrates' court** and demands trial by **jury.** When there is a jury, the **judge's** role is limited to deciding questions of **law,** summing-up to the jury, and, if necessary, sentencing. The jury decides whether the **defendant** is **guilty** or not guilty, based on the **facts.**

The Crown Court hears **appeals** from the **magistrates' court**. It may also hear **civil cases**. There are 94 Crown Courts in England and Wales. The most famous is the **Central Criminal Court** in London, the Old Bailey.

crown immunity

Immunity which the monarch enjoys against all civil or criminal liability, and which government ministers and officials enjoy against some kinds of **prosecution**. For example, it has been held that ministers cannot be in **contempt of court** even if they breach their own undertakings to the **court**.

Crown Prosecution Service

A body independent of the police which considers **evidence** garnered by the police and decides whether to prosecute and on what **charges**. The national head of the service is the **Director of Public Prosecutions** who is responsible to the **Attorney-General,** a **barrister** MP of the party in power. There is no obligation to prosecute when a **crime** has been committed and evidence cited. There could be several reasons for not prosecuting: a **defendant** may be old or ill; he or she may be a small cog in a big operation whose ringleaders cannot be found; the evidence may be good but not enough to get a conviction. The DPP says he works on a 51% rule: there must be a better than even chance of getting a conviction. Other authorities can launch prosecutions, among them the **Inland Revenue,** Customs and Excise, the Department of Social Security and **local authorities.**

See **private prosecution**.

culpable homicide

In Scots law, a killing caused by someone's fault but which lacks the evil intention to be classed as **murder**. It is similar to **manslaughter** in English law.

curator bonis

/ˈkjʊrətə/

In Scotland, an individual appointed to manage the **estate** of a **child** in place of the legal **guardian,** or to manage the estate of an adult suffering from a mental or physical disability.

curtilage

The enclosed area of **land** adjacent to a property.

custody

1 Imprisonment following conviction.

2 An **accused** may be *remanded in custody* (kept at a police station, remand centre or prison) if a **court hearing** is adjourned. Usually a first **remand** in custody lasts 8 days; a court may then order further and longer periods of remand. The accused can apply for release on **bail,** known as being *remanded on bail.*

3 Legal possession, guardianship or control.
See **guardian; parental responsibility.**

D

damages

A **remedy** providing money **compensation** for a **civil wrong**. In breach of **contract cases,** the compensation aims to restore the innocent **parties** to the position they would have enjoyed had the contract been performed as agreed. In **tort** or **delict** the aim is to compensate the **plaintiff** or **pursuers** for the loss actually suffered and to place them in the position they would have been in if the tort or delict had not occurred. Plaintiffs must take **reasonable** steps to lessen their loss, for example by seeking medical treatment if they are injured. Damages may be reduced if the plaintiff's actions contributed to the problem— **contributory negligence.**

damnum

See **delict.**

data protection

Safeguards relating to personal information about individuals that is stored on computer. The rights of such individuals (*data subjects*) and the responsibilities of computer users (*data users*) are set out in the Data Protection Act 1984.

Data users must register their activities with the Data Protection Registrar. Individuals have a right to find out (on payment of a fee) what personal data a data user holds about him or her and to have it corrected or erased if it is wrong or misleading. This right does not extend to information held in paper files. The principles of data protection include:

1 information contained in personal data must be obtained fairly and lawfully;

2 personal data must be processed fairly and lawfully;

3 personal data must not be used or disclosed in a way incompatible with the data user's registered purposes;

4 personal data must be accurate and kept up to date;

5 appropriate security measures must be taken against unauthorized access, alteration and disclosure of the data. This in effect gives the data subject a right to **sue** a data user for inadequate security.

In return for a fee, an individual may apply for and obtain a copy of any criminal convictions recorded against him or her on the UK Police National Computer, using a standard form available from Scotland Yard.

Leaflets issued by the Data Protection Registrar treat *data* as a plural, to the glee of purists.

death duties
Inheritance tax charged on someone's **property** on death.

death penalty
See **capital punishment**.

debtor
A **person** who owes money to a **creditor**. Although debtors' prisons have been abolished, it is still possible to go to prison for debt, for example if you do not pay the correct maintenance money to a former **marriage** partner or fail to pay **fines** or community charge. You cannot, however, go to prison for becoming **bankrupt**.

deceased, the
Someone who is dead.

deception
Making a deliberate or reckless false **representation** about a matter of **fact** or **law;** technically referred to as **deceit**. Deception is not in itself a **crime** unless it is used, for example, to obtain property, services, insurance, an annuity contract, money or extra money in a job, or to win money by betting.

declarator
In Scots law, an **action** seeking to have some right judicially declared but without claim on the **defender** to take any action.

declinature

In Scots law, refusal by a **judge** to try a **case,** perhaps because he or she is related to one of the **parties** or has a financial **interest** in it.

decree

/'diːkriː/

In Scots law, the technical term for a final **court judgment.** The first syllable is stressed.

decree nisi

At the start, every **divorce** decree in England and Wales is a decree nisi, meaning that it is provisional until the end of a fixed period when it becomes *absolute.* During the period anyone may come forward to try to show why the decree should not be made absolute; the couple remain married until it is. At the end of the period the individual who obtained the decree applies for it to be made absolute, when the **marriage** finally ends. A list of decrees absolute is open to the public in the **Divorce Registry.**

deed

1 In England and Wales, a signed, sealed and delivered document intended to give legal force to a wish, agreement etc. **Conveyances, trust instruments, settlements** and **mortgages** may all be set out as deeds. Formerly deeds were of two kinds, *poll* and *indented.* A deed poll, made by one **person,** was so called because the paper was shaved or polled evenly on all sides. A deed indented was made by two or more people. To prevent **fraud** each part was cut or indented in acute angles on the top or side to tally or correspond with the other; hence the words *indenture* and *counterpart.* It is expensive and, for most purposes unnecessary, to use a deed poll to change one's name—a simple declaration will do.

See **change of name; seal.**

2 In Scots law, a deed is a formal legal document which is signed and witnessed by two **witnesses.**

deed of arrangement

A written agreement between a **debtor** and his or her **creditors,** when no **bankruptcy** order has been made. It arranges the debtor's affairs for the benefit of the creditors or, if the debtor is insolvent, for the benefit of at least three creditors.

deed of covenant

See **covenant.**

deed of gift

A **deed** conveying **property** from one **person** to another without any consideration in return.

See **contract.**

deem

To regard something as true even though it may not be: *This document is deemed to have been lodged with the court on the due date.*

deemster or dempster

The title of a **judge** in the Isle of Man.

defamation

The Scots law term for **libel** and **slander.**

default

Failure to do something required by **law.**

default notice

A **notice** that must be served on someone who has broken a **contract** before **action** is taken in response to the breach.

defect

A fault or failing in something. In a sale of goods, a buyer has no legal **remedy** if the defect was **patent,** ie obvious when he or she inspected the goods in the shop. If the defect was not apparent at first, ie was **latent,** the buyer would have a legal remedy.

defective equipment

Faulty tools or equipment provided by an employer for a job. An employer has a duty to provide employees with a safe system of work, so far as reasonably practicable, and can be sued by an injured employee as well as being prosecuted by the Health and Safety Executive.

defence

1 In **civil law,** a **defendant's** answer to a **plaintiff's statement of claim.**

2 In **criminal law,** either the defendant's representatives in court, or the arguments put forward to support the defendant's **plea.**

defendant

The **person** called upon to answer proceedings brought against him or her. In **civil cases,** the defendant is the person being sued by the **plaintiff;** in criminal cases, the defendant is the person accused by the **prosecution.**

defender

In Scots law, the **party** against whom a **civil case** is brought.

delegated legislation

Legislation made under powers given by an **Act of Parliament** (the parent Act). Delegated legislation enables government ministers and **local authorities** to supplement the parent Act with additional legal rules. They must keep strictly to the powers given by the Act otherwise they can be challenged in the courts. This kind of legislation allows details to be added to the broad principles of legislation without the need for a new Act of Parliament.

See **byelaw.**

delict

In Scotland, a **civil wrong** arising from conduct (either fault or **negligence**) which causes loss or injury to someone else. It entitles the **person** concerned to **sue** the offender for **damages,** known as *reparation*. To win damages, the **pursuer** must prove **damnum** (loss or injury), **injuria** (conduct amounting to a legal wrong) and that the conduct caused the injury.

demesne

/dɪ'mem/

In property **law,** the possession and use of one's own **property** or **land.**

de minimis non curat lex

[Latin: The law ignores trifles] A maxim which means that **courts** will not award **damages** for a trivial matter.

demise

To let or grant a **lease** or the lease itself. Thus *the demised premises.*

dependant

In England and Wales, someone who relies on another for **maintenance** or financial support. On the death of the individual depended upon, **courts** have wide powers to make financial provision to dependants out of the **estate**—whatever the individual's **will** may say.

deportation

Expulsion from the UK under the Immigration Act 1971.

descendants

In a **will,** the will-maker's **children,** grandchildren, great grandchildren etc, whether male or female.

desertion

The failure by a husband or wife to live with the **marriage** partner which, if it continues for more than 2 years, may be grounds for **divorce.** Desertion usually means leaving the **matrimonial home** but there may be desertion if all elements of a shared life have ended even though the partners live under the same roof.

detention

In England and Wales, following **arrest,** the deprivation of
someone's liberty against their will. Normally detention of
adults without charge may last up to 24 hours if it is necessary to
secure or preserve **evidence** or to get it by questioning. It can be
prolonged to 36 hours for **serious arrestable offences** if a senior
police officer believes it necessary. Extensions up to a total of 96
hours are possible with a **magistrate's** permission. Under the
Police and Criminal Evidence Act 1984, arrested people
normally have the right to have one individual told of their
arrest, to seek legal advice, to make a phone call, and to receive
visits from friends or relatives if the custody officer agrees.
Terrorism suspects may be held for 48 hours without charge
and this may be extended to 5 days by the Home Secretary.

detention in a youth offender institution

Apart from **custody** for life, this is the only custodial **sentence**
for someone under 21 in England and Wales. The minimum
detention period is 21 days and the maximum, for offenders of
17 and over, is the same as the imprisonment term for the
offence.

determine

Legalese for *end* or *terminate. To determine a contract* is to bring
it to an end or cancel it, usually for some reason stated in the
contract. Hence *determination.*

diet

In Scotland, the date of a **hearing** fixed by the **court.**

diligence

In Scotland, a procedure which enables a **person** who has won
a court **action** to compel the loser to comply with the **court's**
decree. Diligence against earnings can be used to deduct debt
repayments from earnings or pensions.

diminished responsibility

An abnormal state of mind not amounting to insanity, which
provides a special **defence** to the charge of **murder**. It may be

caused by disease, injury or irresistible impulse. If the defence succeeds, the **accused** is convicted of **manslaughter** or culpable homicide.

Diplock courts

Terrorism trials in Northern Ireland which are heard without a **jury** to avoid intimidation. They began in 1973 and are named after Lord Diplock who recommended their use.

diplomatic immunity

The freedom from legal proceedings granted to members of diplomatic missions of foreign states. The extent of the freedom depends on the member's diplomatic status. A diplomat, for example, would normally have almost complete criminal and civil immunity, whereas the immunity of a member of the domestic staff would be limited to matters arising from their official duties. Ambassadors can set aside the immunity of their staff.

direct evidence

Either a **witness's** statement in **court,** offered as proof of the truth of a **fact,** or a witness's **statement** that he or she perceived a fact with one of his or her own senses.

See **circumstantial evidence; hearsay.**

direction to a jury

A **judge's** statements to a **jury** on matters of **law,** such as the definition of the **crime** charged and the nature and scope of possible **defences**. The jury decides on questions of **fact.**

director

A company officer appointed by or under the **articles of association.** In law, directors must use skill and care in discharging their responsibilities. They are obliged to act in good faith for the benefit of the company and the members as a whole, and must not act in an oppressive way to any one section of the members.

When a company's business has been conducted in a dishonest manner which is likely to defraud its **creditors,** a director may be held personally liable to contribute towards the company's assets as well as being disqualified from being a director for up to 15 years. Directors who know, or ought to know, that there is no **reasonable** prospect of a company remaining solvent, must do everything possible to prevent loss to the company's creditors, otherwise their own assets may be at risk. In practice, however, these sanctions are rarely used.

See **limited liability company.**

Director of Public Prosecutions
See **Crown Prosecution Service.**

disabled person
Someone substantially handicapped by injury, disease or deformity from getting or keeping work suitable to his or her age, experience and qualifications. Every employer of 20 or more people must employ a quota of disabled people registered as such with the Department of Employment. Failure to fulfil a quota may be an **offence.**

discharge
To release an **accused** or a prisoner, or to release someone from an obligation.

discharge order
A **court** order which releases a **debtor** from all debts at the end of a **bankruptcy** proceeding. It may be subject to conditions, but normally it releases the debtor from all the legal disabilities he or she has suffered as an **undischarged bankrupt.**

disclosure of documents
In an English **civil case,** the disclosure of relevant documents to the other side. In a **High Court action** begun by a **writ,** disclosure is automatic and mutual—each side serves a list of documents on the other. In other cases, the **court** or **tribunal** will usually order disclosure.

dishonesty

The taking of **property** belonging to someone else with the intention of permanently depriving him or her of it. To convict, the **court** must be satisfied that the action was dishonest by the standards of ordinary, decent people and that the **accused** knew this at the time.

dismissal

The ending of an employee's **contract** of employment by the employer, usually by giving **notice**.

See **unfair dismissal; wrongful dismissal**.

distress (distraint)

The seizing of a wrongdoer's goods by an injured **party** as **security** for the performance of some obligation. For example, a **landlord** might seize a **tenant's** goods to secure payment of rent arrears. If they remain unpaid, the goods can be sold and the proceeds put towards the debt. **Local authorities** and **housing associations** can use distress for rent arrears without getting a **court** order. The **Inland Revenue** and Customs & Excise use distress to recover tax and VAT.

Certain goods cannot be seized: those not personally owned by the **debtor;** those being bought under **hire purchase;** the tools of the debtor's trade; and personal belongings and household goods necessary for everyday life.

In Scotland the analogous procedure is **poinding**.

district court

In Scotland, the lowest rank of criminal **court,** dealing with the less serious **offences** occurring in its locality (known as the *commission area*).

district judge

A **judge** in the **county court,** usually addressed as *Sir* or *Madam*.

divisional court

A **court** in England and Wales presided over by at least two **judges** from a division of the **High Court**. It hears **appeals** and supervises inferior courts.

divorce

The termination by **court** order of a valid **marriage**. English courts now recognize only one ground for divorce: the irretrievable breakdown of **marriage**. This must be supported by one of five **facts**. The individual applying for the divorce (*petitioner*) must show that the other party (**respondent**) has: committed adultery; or displayed unreasonable behaviour; or deserted the petitioner for two years before the divorce petition; or lived apart from the petitioner for 2 years and consented to the divorce; or lived apart for 5 years. Similar grounds for divorce apply in Scotland.

Arrangements concerning **children** and money may be agreed between the **parties** or decided by the court. A divorce will not be given within the first year after the marriage has been made.

In 1989 182 000 couples in the UK divorced.

New proposals (1991) would enable couples to divorce without citing a 'fault' (such as adultery) within a year of their marriage breaking down, provided all matters such as property, money and provision for children had been settled; conciliation would be available if needed.

Divorce Registry

In England and Wales, the section of the Family Division of the **High Court** which has **jurisdiction** over **divorce** proceedings.

DNA tests

[Acronym: Deoxyribonucleic acid, the main constituent of chromosomes] Forensic tests using a small sample of tissue, blood, saliva or semen which enable paternity or identity to be established by showing to which DNA group someone belongs. The use of these tests in paternity **cases** will enable an alleged father to be identified with certainty and thus make him liable to pay **maintenance**.

dole

In Scots law, *evil intention,* roughly comparable to the English law's **mens rea**.

dolus

In Scots law, a trick or falsehood designed to cheat or deceive someone.

domicile

The country in which someone has their fixed or permanent home and to which, when they are absent, they intend to return. In **law,** nobody may have more than one domicile at any one time. Domicile is of three sorts: *by birth*; *by choice*; and *by operation of law.* Domicile matters for various reasons: for example, if someone is domiciled in France and makes a **will** according to the laws of France, an English **court** will recognize its validity even though English legal procedures were not followed.

Compare **residence**.

dominant tenement

Land whose ownership confers a **servitude** right—such as a right of access or a right to receive daylight—over adjoining land, called the **servient tenement**.

dooms

Laws made by Anglo-Saxon kings.

door tenant

A non-practising, but famous, member of a barristers' **chambers** whose main workplace is elsewhere but whose name appears on the posh doorplate close to that of practising members. It's a status symbol for the chambers and a bit like honorary membership for the **barrister** concerned. Nelson Mandela's name adorns a chambers in London.

double jeopardy

The doctrine that no-one may be convicted twice of the same **crime,** or for different crimes arising from the same set of **facts** unless the crimes involve substantially different wrongs. Nor may anyone acquitted of a crime be brought to trial for the same **offence.**

driving licence

An official authority to drive the types of motor vehicle specified on the **licence**. It is granted on passing the driving test relevant to those types. Anyone over the age of 17 can obtain a licence, though there are exceptions including mental illness and bad eyesight (inability to read a number plate at 25 yards while wearing glasses in daylight). Learners first receive a provisional licence. A police officer can demand to see your licence if:

1 you are driving on the road or supervising a learner; or

2 he or she reasonably believes that you have committed a motoring **offence** or are the driver of a vehicle where an accident occurred.

You must either produce your licence on the spot or take it personally to a police station you nominate within 5 days.

drunkenness

In England, it is an **offence,** punishable by **fine,** to be drunk in a public place. Being *drunk and disorderly* attracts a heavier fine. Drunkenness is not a valid **defence** to a **crime** nor is it likely to lessen a **sentence.**

See **intoxication.**

duress

Violence or threats of violence against someone intended to cause him or her to act in a particular way, such as to commit a **crime. Courts** can sometimes set aside **contracts** entered into or altered as a result of duress.

during Her Majesty's pleasure

A phrase formerly used in the **law** to describe the period of detention imposed on a **defendant** found not guilty because of insanity. The individual was as a result known as a *pleasure patient.*

duty of care

The legal obligation to take **reasonable** care to avoid causing **damage.** Doctors have a duty of care to their patients, as do drivers to other road users, and **solicitors** to their **clients**. A breach of a duty of care can give rise to a civil claim for **negligence**.

It is not clear whether professionals owe different duties of care according to their qualifications and experience. Until recently, **courts** had ruled that all qualified doctors owed patients a similar duty of care. In 1990 this view was jeopardized in a **case** which went to the **Court of Appeal**. A firm of provincial auctioneers had valued two grubby oil paintings of foxhounds at £30–50 and the owners were pleased when they fetched £840 at auction. Pleasure turned to dismay when the picture realized £88 000 at Sotheby's after an acute dealer spotted that they were in the style of the famous George Stubbs. The Court of Appeal ruled that the provincial auctioneers and their consultant valuer were not negligent because their limited experience in the provinces meant they owed a lower duty of care than if the owners had approached a London auction house.

This opens the possibility that a learner driver could be regarded as owing a lower duty of care to other road users than an experienced driver, and that a newly qualified surgeon might have a lower duty of care to a patient than an experienced one.

duty solicitors

Solicitors who attend **magistrates' courts** by rota to help **defendants** who would otherwise go unrepresented.

E

easement

A right exercised by one landowner over the **land** of another. The easement must benefit the land of its owner and it ends if both **properties** (the **dominant** and **servient tenements**) are later owned and occupied by one owner. Easements may be stated in writing, implied, or acquired through long use (known as *prescription*). Types of easement include the taking of water, the support of buildings and **ancient lights**. Easements cannot be used to protect certain things, such as an unspoilt view, though a **restrictive covenant** against building may achieve the desired effect. A private **right of way** may exist as an easement, though a **person** may instead have permission to cross the land under a **licence**.

Easement came to English from Old French in the 14th century, when it meant being eased from pain, then changed in meaning to comfort or enjoyment. In the 15th century the term meant a privy or a bowel movement.

See **light or prospect**.

eavesdrop

[Old English *yfesdrype:* water dripping from the eaves] The Scots law term for the burden imposed on a **servient tenement** of receiving the drippings from the eaves of the **dominant tenement**. Also called *stillicide*.

edictal citation

In Scots law, a way of citing someone who is abroad to appear as a witness or juror, for example.

Edinburgh Gazette

The official publication of the government in Scotland. It contains government notices and information about the acts of the Queen in her political capacity.

effeiring to
In Scotland, *relating to.*

effluxion of time
The passage of time. An unusual term, almost extinct even among **lawyers,** though it appeared in a council circular to residents in the mid-1980s: *A landlord must not less than 4 weeks before the expiry by effluxion of time of any tenancy which expires without the service of any notice to quit, notify the council in writing that the tenancy is about to expire in accordance with the said schedule.*

See **expiration.**

eggshell skull rule
The rule that a wrongdoer cannot expect a lesser **charge** or lighter **sentence** if the injuries he or she caused were more serious than expected because the victim had a pre-existing weakness, such as a very thin skull.

eik

/iːk/

In Scots law, an addition to an **executor's** inventory of a **deceased's estate,** so as to include additional **property.**

eiusdem generis
[Latin: of the same kind] A rule used when interpreting a list of things in a legal document. If a list of specific things belonging to the same class is followed by general words, a **court** will restrict the meaning of the general words to other things in that class. For example, in a tenancy agreement which restricts the ownership of pets to *cats, budgerigars, hamsters and other animals,* the general words would mean *other domestic animals.* So the **tenant** could keep a pet dog or rabbit but not a tiger or a venomous snake.

election
Choosing by vote a member of a representative body.

elector
>Someone entitled to vote at **elections**.

electronic surveillance
>Obtaining **evidence** by secret electronic means such as hidden microphones or cameras. Such evidence can normally be used in **court** proceedings.
>
>See **telephone tapping**.

embezzlement
>The dishonest taking of money or other **property** entrusted to an employee on behalf of the employer. It is classed as **theft** under English law, though Scots law distinguishes it from theft and **fraud**.

emergency protection order
>A **court** order for the protection of **children** at risk of significant harm if they are not removed from a place or if they do not remain in a place. The order lasts for up to 8 days.

emoluments
>Earnings from salaries, fees, wages, profits etc.

employee's inventions
>Things and techniques invented by an employee during work for the employer. These usually belong to the employer, though the employee may be awarded **compensation** by the Comptroller General of Patents, Designs and Trademarks if the invention provides the employer with outstanding benefit.

Employment Appeal Tribunal
>A **statutory body,** chaired by a **High Court judge,** which hears **appeals** on questions of **law** (not matters of **fact**) from **industrial tribunals**. It is a court not a tribunal, though its procedures are relatively informal—robes are not worn, there is no **bench** or **witness** box and the court can be addressed without standing up. Witnesses can be called and the **disclosure of documents** ordered. **Costs** are not usually awarded

against the loser. **Legal aid** is available. The court can be held anywhere in the country and its **judgments** can be enforced.

encumbrance

A right or **interest** in **land** owned by someone who does not own the land. An example is the interest of a building society in land on which it lends money under a **mortgage**. Encumbrances are usually registered at the **Land Registry,** then they become binding on buyers of the land.

endorsement

1 The noting of a driving **offence** on a **driving licence**.

2 An extra clause or **condition** noted on an **insurance policy,** which becomes part of the policy.

enforcement notice

A **notice** requiring certain steps to be taken within a specified time to **remedy** an alleged breach of, for example, planning control or health and safety **law.**

engagement to marry

A spoken or written agreement to marry at a future date. This is not an enforceable **contract**. Engagement rings are absolute gifts and need not be returned when an engagement is broken. If the engaged couple were buying a house when the engagement was broken, their **property** rights would be decided in accordance with those that govern married couples. Any wedding presents would normally be returned to the senders.

English, use of

See **legalese; sentence, length of; Statute of Pleading.**

engross

To get a document complete and ready for signature.

enjoy

In legal writing, to *possess or have.* So *he enjoys the right of access* just means *he has the right of access,* not that he experiences pleasure whenever he uses it.

See **quiet enjoyment.**

entering judgment

A procedure for recording a **civil court's** formal decision.

entrapment

Deliberately trapping someone into committing a **crime** so as to obtain a conviction. English **courts**, unlike those in the US, do not permit a **defence** of entrapment—the **accused** is considered to be still capable of exercising free will. However, entrapment may restrict the kind of evidence a **judge** allows, and may help to lessen a **sentence**.

equal pay

See **sex discrimination**.

equity

A source of English and Scottish **law** which began developing in the 15th century. When a petitioner could not find a procedurally acceptable way of using the **common law,** he would take his allegation of injustice to the monarch by means of a **petition**. As the number of petitions swelled, the **Lord Chancellor** started to decide **cases** in the monarch's name without using a rigid rule of law but relying on common sense and **natural justice**. The Court of Chancery took over this function and by the 19th century had developed a body of **precedent,** buttressed by a set of fixed principles, known as equity.

Today the Chancery Division in English law has **jurisdiction** over much equity work, such as **trust** law and some kinds of **injunction**. Modern equity provides a supplementary system of law, using moral ideas like fairness, natural justice and good conscience to help decide cases. It is still tied, however, to the doctrine of precedent.

Scotland has never had such a separation between common law and equity. The term therefore has different connotations in Scotland, where it tends to mean fairness, reasonableness, natural justice and the ability to provide a **remedy** where **justice** requires it and none is otherwise available.

escape

In **common law,** it is an **offence** to escape without force from lawful **custody** (which need not be a prison or even a building) or to help a prisoner to escape. Escape using force is the offence of *prison breaking.*

escrow

/'ɛskroʊ or ɛ'skroʊ/

Money, goods or a document delivered to a **third party** who holds it until some **condition** is met. For example, a booking agency taking your money for a theatre ticket might hold it *in escrow* until you receive the ticket from the theatre.

ESDA

[Acronym: Electrostatic Deposition Analysis] A system of analysing sheets of notepaper to see whether they were written upon consecutively or whether some were inserted afterwards. The system has been used for some years by **forensic scientists** on behalf of the **prosecution.** It has come to be used by the **defence** when trying to show that police have distorted **statements** and **confessions** by inserting fresh sheets bearing fictitious remarks by the **accused.**

estate

1 In revenue law, the total of all the **property** to which someone is entitled.

2 In **land** law, the character and duration of someone's ownership of land.

See **leasehold; freehold.**

estate agent

An agent concerned with the sale, leasing, valuation and management of **property.**

Anyone may set up as an estate agent, regardless of qualifications or experience. By **law,** agents must tell clients in writing if they have a personal interest in the sale or purchase of property. They must not give inaccurate or misleading information about **properties,** nor discriminate against buyers who refuse tie-in services such as arranging their **mortgage**. They must tell sellers if they are offering tie-in services to potential buyers. Agents must not invent or give misleading information about potential buyers and must pass on all offers promptly. They must give clients written **notice** of their fees in advance.

If an agent breaks these rules, consumers can complain to a local trading standards department or direct to the Office of Fair Trading. Rogue agents can be banned or fined. There is no national complaints and **compensation** scheme, though some of the bigger agencies take part in an **ombudsman** scheme which can award up to £100,000 compensation.

estoppel

[Old French: a stopper or bung] A rule preventing someone from denying the truth of a **statement** they have made or from denying **facts** they have alleged to exist. Anyone taking a **civil action** for estoppel would usually have to show that they had acted upon the statement of fact to their own disadvantage. There are several kinds of estoppel, for example: *by record,* which prevents people denying a **court judgment** against them; and *by deed,* which says that a signatory to a **deed** cannot deny what is stated in the deed.

In Scotland the analogous term is **personal bar.**

European Communities (or European Community)

A grouping which comprises the European Economic Community (EEC), the European Coal and Steel Community (ECSC) and the European Atomic Energy Community (EURATOM). The EEC is an economic alliance of Belgium, Holland, Luxembourg, France, Germany, Italy, UK, Denmark, Greece, Republic of Ireland, Spain and Portugal. The same member states form the ECSC and EURATOM.

See **community law**.

European Community Directive

A piece of legislation made by the **Council of Ministers of the European Communities** requiring member states of **European**

Communities to adapt their own **laws** so as to achieve the result specified in the Directive. If a member state fails to do so, **persons** intended to benefit from the Directive can rely on it in legal **action** against public sector bodies like government departments, local authorities and health authorities. The Commission of the European Communities can also take legal action against the government of a member state that fails to comply with a Directive by the due date. This can result in the state being taken before the **European Court of Justice** although the court cannot fine states, merely declare them in breach.

European Community Regulation

A piece of legislation made by the **Council** or **Commission of the European Communities** and which applies directly as **law** in the member states.

European Convention on Human Rights

See **Court of Human Rights**.

European Court of Justice

See **community law**.

European Parliament

An assembly directly elected by citizens entitled to vote in each of the member states. Members (MEPs) sit in political not regional groups. The European Parliament supervises the legislative and administrative activities of the **Council** or **Commission of the European Communities**. The Council (or occasionally the Commission) must consult or seek co-operation from the European Parliament before passing **European Community law**.

eviction

The removal of a **tenant** or occupier from occupation. It is an **offence** to evict residential occupiers without a **court** order or to harass them into leaving. Anyone unlawfully evicted may claim **damages**.

See **harassment**.

evidence

Whatever tends to prove the truth in **court**, for example sworn testimony or documentary **evidence**.

See **circumstantial evidence; direct evidence**.

examination-in-chief

The questioning of **witnesses** in **court** by the **party** who called them to give **evidence**.

excambion

In Scotland, *exchange of lands*.

exclusion order

A **court** order to exclude or dispossess someone from **property** to which they otherwise have a legal right.

execution

1 The carrying out of a death **sentence** imposed by a **court**.

2 The completion of a **deed** or **will** to make it legally valid.

3 The enforcement of the rights of a **creditor** or other **litigant**, supported by a court **judgment**; this may be by **writ** or **warrant**. A word associated with the death penalty makes ordinary legal **notices** sound more frightening than they are, as in this notice to a group of pickets: *If you neglect to obey this order in the time referred to herein, you will be liable to process of execution for the purpose of propelling you to obey the same.*

See **herein; same**.

executor

Someone appointed by a **will** to administer the **deceased's** property after death and carry out their deceased's wishes. *Executrix* means the female of the species.

In Scots law, an *executor nominate* is the executor named in a will; an *executor dative* is appointed by the **court**.

exemplary damages

In **civil law**, damages awarded by a **court** to punish a **defendant**, over and above the sum awarded to compensate the **plaintiff** for harm done. Exemplary damages are rare (and generally confined to **defamation)** but they are often mentioned in **solicitors'** letters in an attempt to frighten an opponent.

ex gratia

[Latin: from favour] Given as a matter of favour rather than out of legal necessity. Hence a club might award an ex gratia payment to an official who had performed some special service beyond the call of duty.

exhibit

An object or document shown to a **witness** in court or referred to in an **affidavit**. Also used as a verb to mean *produced along with* as in *The document is exhibited to my affidavit.*

ex officio

[Latin: by virtue of office] A club president or treasurer might be a member of the club committee because of the office they hold: they are *ex officio members.*

exemption clause

A term in a **contract** whereby one **party** seeks to exclude or limit liability for obligations arising under the contract.

ex parte

[Latin: of the one part] 1 An ex parte **injunction** is one granted after hearing only one side in the **case.**

2 When the term precedes a name in the heading of a **law report,** it refers to the party on whose application the case is heard.

expenses

The Scots law term for the **costs** of an **action.**

expiration

Legalese for *expiry* or *the end of a period of time,* as in *Where the tribunal refuse to defer the operation of a notice to quit, the notice does not have effect before the expiration of 7 days after the date* *of the tribunal's decision,* an example which also exposes the **lawyer's** love of multiple negatives.

expire

End or *come to an end.*

extract

In Scots law, a formal copy of a legal document, such as a copy of a **court decree**.

extradition

The surrender by country A to country B of someone accused of an **offence** in B. There must be an extradition treaty between the two countries. In UK law, the offence must: be a **crime** in both countries; be covered specifically by the treaty; fall within the list of extraditable offences in the Extradition Act 1870; and be non-political.

F

factor

In Scotland, a manager acting on behalf of an owner of **heritage**.

facts

Events or circumstances known to have existed or happened.

failure to maintain

The failure of a **marriage** partner to provide **reasonable maintenance** for the other or contribute properly towards the **children** of the family while the marriage lasts. **Courts** can order payments to be made.

fair rent

The rent registered for a **property** occupied by a **secure** or **regulated tenant**. The amount is set by a rent officer or rent assessment committee in relation to the type and quality of the property without regard to its open market value.

false accounting

The **offence** of dishonestly falsifying, destroying or hiding an account or document used in accounting, or using it knowing it to be false or misleading. The offence is committed if it creates a gain or causes loss to someone.

false pretence

A deliberate false **statement** of **fact** which cheats or defrauds someone of money or **property**. The **offence** is now known as *obtaining property by deception*. The term *false pretences* still exists in the offence of successfully persuading a woman to have **sexual intercourse** by false pretences; it is punishable by up to 2 years in prison.

Family Division

A **High Court** division dealing with **divorce,** other domestic business, and uncontentious **probate** matters.

fatal accident

An accident in which death occurs, though *accident* is not defined in **law.** The **estate** of someone killed in an accident can **sue** and be sued for **negligence** and any **damages** are added to or subtracted from the **estate.** Close dependants of someone who is killed can bring an action for negligence and attempt to win damages for loss of the financial support they could have expected to receive from him or her. In some circumstances damages for bereavement and funeral expenses can be claimed.

fatal accident inquiry

In Scotland, an inquiry into death where there is **reasonable** cause to suspect violence or unnatural death. The inquiry is presided over by a **sheriff** and conducted by the **procurator fiscal.**

fee

In Scots law, the full right of **property** in **land** and houses. Its owner is a *fiar.*

Compare **liferent.**

fee simple

See **freehold; leasehold.**

feu

/fju:/

In Scotland, an area of **land** held under a feudal tenure. The **person** who feus the land is a *superior.* The holder is a *vassal* or *feuar* /'fjʊəʳ/. Land ownership in Scotland is still basically feudal: in theory the land belongs to the monarch, landowners deriving their right to own it directly or indirectly through the monarch's permission.

feu duty

In Scotland, the regular amount paid by a vassal to a superior.

See **feu**.

fiar

See **fee**.

fiduciary relationships

Relationships arising from the trust and confidence which one side places in the other. Examples include **solicitor** and **client, guardian** and ward, company **director** and shareholders. Serious breaches of trust might create a right to take legal **action** or complain to the trustee's professional association.

fieri facias (fi. fa.)

[Latin: you must cause to be made] A **writ** directing the **sheriff** to seize enough of the **debtor's** goods to cover the amount of the **judgment** awarded against him or her.

file, client's

The file of papers which a **solicitor** holds about a **client's case**. The papers in this file belong to the client. If the client decides to change solicitors, the solicitor should hand over the file within a **reasonable** time. The client should normally be able to inspect the file at any reasonable time, though many **litigants** find it easier to keep their own copy of important documents; solicitors have been known to lose files and important papers from them.

file, court

The **court** record of a **case**, containing original documents such as **affidavits**.

fine

A sum of money a **court** may order an offender to pay on conviction. The amount is on a graduated scale according to the seriousness of the **offence** but is also affected by the offender's means. A fine may be imposed on top of or instead of another **sentence**.

firearm

Any potentially lethal barrelled weapon capable of firing a shot, bullet or other missile, or any weapon classified for use by the armed forces and having no normal use in everyday life. The main firearms **offences** are: buying or possessing a firearm without a **licence;** carrying a firearm and suitable ammunition in a public place without good excuse; possessing a firearm with intent to endanger life or using it to resist or prevent a lawful **arrest;** buying or hiring a firearm under the age of 17; carrying or using an imitation firearm with criminal intent.

fire-raising

The Scots law term for **arson.**

fish royal

Sturgeon and whale which, when thrown ashore or caught near the coast, belong to the Crown.

fit for purpose

A standard that a trader's goods must meet in a sale to a private customer. If they don't meet this standard, the trader is breaking the **contract** and the customer can get a refund or **sue** for **damages.** If customers say they have a particular purpose in mind for the goods, then the trader sells them with the implied **condition** that they are fit for that purpose.

See **merchantable quality; satisfactory quality.**

fixture

An object which is regarded for legal purposes as having become part of—annexed to—the **land** or **property.** The degree and purpose of the annexation are relevant in deciding whether the object is a fixture or remains the property of the **person** selling the land or property. When moving house, it is best for the **contract** to specify exactly what is a fixture, to be left for the incoming occupier, and what is a fitting, to be removed by the seller. This is necessary in view of the meanness of some sellers in removing light bulbs and digging up garden shrubs.

flag of convenience

A flag of a country other than the shipowner's own, to which the shipowner transfers registration of the vessel in order to avoid taxation, employ cheaper crews and avoid safety regulations.

footpath

Any **highway** over which the public have a **right of way** on foot only. It differs from a *footway,* which is part of a highway that includes a way for vehicles. Footpaths must be at least a metre wide, 1.5 metres for a field-edge path. It is an **offence** to interfere with a footpath in any way that makes it inconvenient to use; so, although farmers may plough their paths, they must restore them within 14 days. The maximum fine for obstructing a footpath is £400.

A field-edge path is sacrosanct and must not be disturbed, except for essential engineering or excavation.

A **bridleway** is a path for pedestrians and horses only; the rights of users are similar to those for footpaths.

The **local authority** must keep a map showing the location and classification of every public right of way. If a path is marked on the map, that is conclusive evidence that it is open to the public, but a path may still be public even if it is not marked on the map. New footpaths can be created. A footpath cannot be lost by disuse, but only by a legal order.

force and fear

The Scots law term for **duress,** which may nullify a **contract.**

force majeure

[French] Irresistible compulsion or coercion. Often used in **contracts** to describe events beyond the control of the **parties.**

foreclosure

The loss of a mortgaged **property** occurring when the **person** who grants the **mortgage** (*the mortgagee*) calls in the loan following a failure to make repayments by the contracted date. The mortgagee first gets a **High Court** order fixing a date for payment. If payment is not made by then, the property belongs to the mortgagee.

See **power of sale.**

foregoing

What has recently been said. A document might refer to *the foregoing provisions of this paragraph.* This puts the reader to the trouble of looking back to see what is meant, and often it's not at all clear. Careful legal writers specify what they mean either by using the words again or by specifying the paragraph by number.

forensic scientists

People who deal with the scientific aspects of detective work, analysing fingerprints and specimens of blood etc. Their usual role is to frame **evidence** for the **prosecution,** so they tend to develop a close working relationship with the police; indeed, most forensic scientists work for the **Home Office** and the Ministry of Defence, and there are few 'independents'. Calls for a fully independent forensic service have followed the disclosure that forensic evidence has sometimes been distorted to fit the prosecution's **case** and has been withheld from the **defence.**

forgery

The **offence** of making a false **instrument** in order to pass it off as genuine, with the intention of defrauding others. The instrument may be a document, Post Office stamp, or device on which information is recorded or stored. The instrument is regarded as false if it seems to have been made or altered on the authority of someone who did not actually give authority or by someone who does not exist, or on a date or at a place when authority was not properly given. It is an offence to reproduce British currency notes, for example by photocopying them or using them in artwork.

formbooks

Books of standard forms which **lawyers** plunder to develop their own documents when they lack the time or skill to write their own. The forms are said to benefit from having 'stood the test of time' and of having 'been tested in the courts', though often the individual words have never been litigated upon. Formbook editors have tended to favour archaic language but this is changing slowly. Material is usually contributed by **solicitors** and **barristers.**

forthwith

An imprecise word in legal documents which means *immediately, fairly soon* or *within a reasonable time,* depending on the context. As the word is ambiguous and has caused endless litigation, careful **lawyers** specify a time limit instead.

forum non conveniens

[Latin: court not appropriate] A **plea** which, if successful, leads the **court** to refuse to exercise **jurisdiction.** The plea may be used if there is some foreign element in the **case** and there is a wish to see the case tried elsewhere.

foster child

A **child** cared for by someone other than its natural or adopted parents. By **law, local authorities** must supervise foster children's welfare within their area and inspect foster homes.

foster parent

Someone who looks after a **foster child.** Foster parents have few legal rights over the **children** they foster although they can apply to have a child made a **ward of court** and ask for **parental responsibility.** Foster children may be removed from the care of foster parents by those who have parental responsibility. However, if a child has lived with foster parents for at least 12 months, they can apply to adopt.

franglais

Considered a recent invention, this now-humorous mingling of English and French was common in the 16th century as **law** reporters tried to jot down in French, the language of law reporting, what was being said in **court** in English. Thus an unfortunate prisoner was said to have *ject un Brickbat a le dit*

Justice que narrowly mist, & pur ceo immediately fuit Indictment drawn per Noy envers le Prisoner, & son dexter manus ampute & fix al Gibbet sur que luy mesme immediatement hange in presence de Court. Brutal times.

fraud

A false statement (or conduct) made knowingly or without belief in its truth; the **fact** that there may have been no intention to cheat anyone is irrelevant. Someone whose interests are injured by fraud may bring an **action** to recover **damages** for deceit. The innocent **party** can **avoid** any **contract** induced by fraud. Fraud is an element in a number of **offences,** such as *obtaining money by deception.*

freehold

Absolute ownership of **land.** Also called *fee simple absolute in possession.*

See **leasehold.**

full committal

In Scotland, the act of sending someone for trial in a criminal matter before a **jury,** following a preliminary **hearing** before a **sheriff.**

furnish

To supply, provide or give. A pompous term still used in modern **Acts of Parliament** like the Courts and Legal Services Act 1990.

furth of

Scots for *outside the borders of.*

G

garnishee order

In England and Wales, a **court** order which requires a **third party** to pay money to a **creditor** who has obtained a court **judgment** against a **debtor**. If the debtor were earning £400 a week, his employer could be ordered to extract, say, £200 a week from his pay packet and pass it to the creditor.

generality

An ambiguous word meaning *general effect* or *majority,* as in this phrase in a will: *without prejudice to the generality of the foregoing provisions.*

general meeting

A meeting of company members whose decisions can bind the company.

ghet

A Jewish religious **divorce** performed by the husband giving a handwritten bill of divorce to his wife in the presence of two **witnesses.** It is only recognized in the UK if it takes place outside the UK, Channel Islands or Isle of Man.

give, devise and bequeath

A long-winded way of saying *give,* often found in **wills.** *Give* and *bequeath* were Old English synonyms for *making a gift* whereas *devise* was Old French for *to divide.* After the Norman Conquest English found itself with surplus words so **lawyers** bracketed all three words together, hoping for certainty.

Many lawyers believe that *devise* refers to the giving of **land** while *bequeath* means the giving of **personal property.** This distinction has never been maintained consistently and there has been endless **litigation** about what the two words mean. *Give,* on the other hand, applies unambiguously to the giving of any **property;** it is therefore the favourite for **lawyers** who want to be clear.

golden rule

A rule used when interpreting **Acts of Parliament.** It says that ordinary words in an Act bear their ordinary meanings while technical words bear their technical meanings, unless this would produce absurdity or a result at variance with **Parliament's** intention.

See **interpretation; literal rule.**

goodwill

The value of the reputation and trade connections of the business, whether in its place of business or through its name. Described by Lord Eldon in 1810 as '[The] probability that the old customers will resort to the old place.' It could be worth a considerable sum on the sale of the business. The seller is usually therefore prohibited by agreement from setting up a rival business for a certain period in competition with the business he or she has sold.

grant of representation

A **court** order which enables the **executor** of a **will,** or the administrator if there is no will, to deal with the **estate** of the **deceased.**

Great Britain

England, Scotland and Wales.

green form

A form used to apply for legal advice and assistance, completed by the **client** and the **solicitor.** The solicitor decides whether the client's means fall within the limits of the scheme and, if so, is entitled to give advice and assistance and recover costs up to the value of £50 from the **legal aid** fund.

grievous bodily harm

See **bodily harm.**

gross indecency

An unlawful sexual act beyond ordinary **indecency** but short of **sexual intercourse**. It may include masturbation and usually involves physical contact, though it need not. It is an **offence** to commit an act of gross indecency with or towards a child under 14. It is an offence for a man to commit an act of gross indecency with another man unless both are over 21, consent, and do it in private.

See **buggery**.

ground rent

A rent payable on a long lease of **land**. When, for example, a house, flat or building plot is sold on a 99 or 999 year lease, the lessor (seller) may charge a small rent payable throughout the term. The occupier can normally buy out the ground rent.

See **leasehold**.

guarantor

One who guarantees to pay a debt if the **debtor** does not pay.

guard dog

A dog kept specifically to protect people or **property** or someone who is guarding them. It is an **offence** to use a guard dog unless it is under the control of a handler or properly secure. An owner may be criminally liable for injury caused by such a dog and can be sued in the **civil courts** for injury caused.

guardian

Someone who looks after the interests of a minor (**child** under 18 in England and Wales, under 16 in Scotland), and has **parental responsibility** towards it. The **courts** may appoint a guardian if a minor has no parent or guardian. A parent or guardian can appoint someone to act as guardian in the event of his or her death, though the appointment must usually be written, dated and signed.

guardian ad litem

[Latin *ad litem*: for the suit] A guardian who protects a **child's** interests in **court** proceedings such as **adoption**. The guardian may be the child's usual guardian, if any, or be appointed by the court. Under the Children Act 1989, virtually all **children in care** and related proceedings have the benefit of a guardian ad litem and a **solicitor** to help the court reach its decisions. The guardian may be required to take part in a court review of the **case**.

guilty

1 An **accused's** admission in **court** that he or she has committed the **offence**.

2 A **verdict** that the accused has committed the offence as charged or some other offence which the **evidence** can support.

guilty knowledge

See **mens rea**.

H

habeas corpus

[Latin: you have the body] In English law, a **writ** requiring someone who detains another (whether privately or by the power of the state) to appear in **court** and justify the detention. If the court considers the detention unreasonable, release is ordered. Dickens rhymingly referred to the writ as a 'have his carcase'.

habit and repute

In Scots civil law, the reputation of being married which, coupled with **cohabitation,** is equivalent to **marriage**. It is known as *irregular marriage* and can be fully established by **decree** of the **Court of Session** after application by one of the partners.

hacking

Gaining unauthorized entry by electronic means to a computer system. If the hacker causes damage, he or she may be prosecuted for *criminal damage*. There could also be a **prosecution** for **abstracting electricity**.

hamesucken

In Scots law, an **assault** on someone in their own home. The **courts** regard it as more serious than mere assault.

handling

Dishonestly receiving things that one knows or believes to be stolen. The **offence** extends to arranging or helping someone to keep, remove or dispose of the things.

Hansard

The nickname for the Official Report of Parliamentary Debates, after the Hansard family, printers to the House of Commons in the 19th century. Hansard provides an almost verbatim record of debates in the Commons and Lords and is published daily and weekly by HMSO. Speakers in debates can correct statements attributed to them but are not supposed to make other changes.

harassment

1 of **debtors:** behaviour intended to force a debtor to pay up. It is an **offence** if the debt is based on a **contract** and the harassment alarms, distresses or humiliates the debtor (for example, the frequent parking of a van marked 'debt collector' outside the debtor's house).

2 of occupiers: the offence of making threats, offering violence or exerting pressure by or on behalf of a **landlord** to get possession of a **property** from a **tenant**. It would be an offence for the landlord to cut off gas, electricity or water even if bills had not been paid.

headnote

The summary at the start of a **law report;** known in Scotland as the *rubric.*

hearing

The trial of a **case** in **court.** In general all cases, whether civil or criminal, are held in public.

See **in camera.**

hearsay

Evidence not actually perceived by **witnesses** with one of their own senses, but claimed or proved by them to have been stated by someone else. In **civil cases,** most hearsay **statements** are admissible in court. In criminal cases they are generally inadmissible though there are exceptions such as the dying declarations of victims of **murder** or **manslaughter** ('My brother Fred did it'), or in sexual abuse cases where **children's** evidence can be used without their testifying in **court.**

Opinion evidence is often allowed in court—a non-expert witness might testify about someone's supposed age, authenticity of handwriting, speed of a car, or identity. Expert witnesses such as doctors might give opinions on matters within their expertise. The **Law Commission** has advocated relaxation on admitting hearsay in criminal cases.

The word is from Old English. **Lawyers** borrowed it from common speech, where it had no technical meaning, in the 16th century.

held

Law report shorthand which prefaces the decision of the **court,** as in *held: the defendant was negligent.*

hereby

Imprecise **legalese** which means *by means of this document* or *right now by means of this document.* The phrase *I hereby give notice* means nothing more than *I give notice.* **Lawyers** uneasy without their usual prop might prefer to say *This document gives notice.* In any case, hereby is redundant—it conveys **legal flavouring** but nothing of substance.

hereditament

In **local authority** rating **law,** a unit of assessment for levying a rate on a property. A *mixed hereditament* is a house-cum-shop, helpfully defined by one local authority's rates bill as: *a hereditament which is not a dwelling house but in the case of which the proportion of the rateable value of the hereditament attributable to the part of the hereditament used for the purposes of a private dwelling is greater than the proportion thereof attributable to the part used for other purposes.*

herein

An imprecise word which may mean *in this document* or *in this section of the document.* The word has caused **litigation** for centuries, so it is surprising that **lawyers** find its use so comforting. Careful lawyers write *in this paragraph* or *in this contract* etc.

hereinafter

Imprecise **legalese** which may mean *in the rest of this document* or *in the rest of this section.* The word is shunned by careful legal writers who prefer to be specific: *in paragraph 10* or *in this document* etc.

herewith
Legalese for *with this.* **Lawyers** often use it tautologously: *I enclose herewith.*

heritage (or heritable property)
In Scots law, **property** in the form of **land** and houses.

Her Majesty's Inspectorate of Police
A body of senior police officers, based in the **Home Office,** which carries out annual inspections of all English and Welsh police forces.

High Court of Justice
The three divisions of the Supreme Court: Queen's Bench, Chancery, and Family. The High Court hears mainly **civil cases** but deals with **appeals** in civil and criminal **cases** on points of **law** from **magistrates' courts**. It also undertakes **judicial review.**

highway
A road or other way over which the public may pass by right, including **footpaths,** bridle ways and navigable rivers.

See **obstruction.**

hire
A **contract** in which ownership of the goods does not pass to the hirer.

hire purchase
A way of buying goods in which purchasers take possession when they pay the first instalment (deposit) and own them on paying the last. Purchasers therefore have no right to sell the goods until the last instalment is paid. Hire purchase transactions are governed by the Consumer Credit Act 1974.

Home Office
The government department which is responsible throughout England and Wales for law and order. Its minister is the Home

Secretary. The Home Office deals with police matters, security services like **MI5,** prisons, the fire services, **nationality,** immigration, race relations, deportation and **extradition**.

homicide

The action of killing another individual.

In England and Wales, *unlawful homicide* includes **murder, manslaughter** and **infanticide.** Rarely, homicide may be lawful, for example in **self defence,** to defend others or to prevent **crime,** but the force used must be **reasonable** in the circumstances. *Excusable homicide* refers to the killing of another human being by accident, when no **negligence** is involved.

In Scots law, homicide may be *casual*—where the killer behaved lawfully, was not careless, and killed unintentionally. *Involuntary culpable homicide* is killing which is not intentional nor grossly **reckless.** *Voluntary culpable homicide* means murder under mitigating circumstances.

But, as one jurist put it, one is equally dead whatever the means.

See **plea in mitigation**.

homologate

In Scots law, to approve and thereby validate a defective **contract,** for example.

homosexuality

Sexual behaviour between people of the same sex. Sexual behaviour between women (*lesbianism*) is not a **crime. Sexual intercourse** between consenting males over 21 is not a crime. **Home Office** figures show that police are more likely to prosecute a man over 21 who has consensual sex with an 18-year-old man than one who has sex with a girl under 16 (the **age of consent**), where a **caution** is often given instead. **Marriage** between homosexuals of the same sex is unlawful in the **United Kingdom.** Intentional promotion of **homosexuality** by **local authorities** is outlawed. This may extend as far as prohibiting plays about homosexuality from council premises, distributing teaching materials about homosexuality in a local education authority's schools or discussing it at school.

See **buggery; gross indecency.**

House of Commons

The Lower House of **Parliament** consisting of 650 elected members (*MPs*). Those who cannot be MPs include people under 21, civil servants, members of the police and regular armed forces, peers, most clergy, convicted prisoners, and the holders of most judicial and public offices.

House of Lords

The Upper House of **Parliament** consisting of about 1 200 unelected Lords Spiritual and Temporal. The spiritual ones are the Archbishops of Canterbury and York, the Bishops of Durham, York and Winchester, and 21 other Anglican bishops. The temporal ones are hereditary peers, life peers, and the Law Lords—11 people holding high judicial rank who carry out the legal functions of the House. The Law Lords (also known as the Lords of Appeal in Ordinary), deal with **appeals** to the House of Lords, acting as the final appeal court in England and Wales for civil and criminal **cases.** In Scotland, the final appeal court is the High Court of Justiciary.

housing association

A not-for-profit organization whose main aim is to provide housing.

Howard League for Penal Reform

An independent charity which works for a more efficient and humane criminal justice system, including better prison conditions. It seeks a freeze on prison building, the appointment of a prison **ombudsman,** the non-imprisonment of fine defaulters, an end to enforced cell-sharing in prisons, and the development of informal ways to solve conflict so that the police and **courts** do not become involved in minor disputes. The league bears the name of John Howard, the 18th century prison reformer.

howsoever

Legalese for *in whatever way; however.*

human rights

Rights and freedoms to which everyone is entitled, though there is no consensus on what these are. The United Nations Universal Declaration of Human Rights (1948) sets out the main rights but is not binding in **international law**. The International Covenant on Civil and Political Rights (1966) and the International Covenant on Economic, Social and Cultural Rights (1966) bind those few countries who have signed them.

See **European Court of Human Rights.**

hypothec

In Scots law, a right in security over a **debtor's** assets, valid even if the debtor still possesses the assets. A **landlord** would have a hypothec for rent over the **tenant's** assets on the rented premises.

I

ignorance of the law is no excuse

A doctrine which says that ignorance of the **law** is no **defence** to criminal or other proceedings. In other words, citizens are presumed to know every detail of the law. This is what lawyers call a **legal fiction,** something assumed to be true even though everyone knows it isn't. While most people can be expected to know something about the main criminal **offences,** they are hardly likely to keep up with the minutiae of the **civil law** or even subtle shifts in judicial opinion about certain criminal offences. Nevertheless, as John Selden said in 1689: 'Ignorance of the law excuses no man; not that all men know the law, but because 'tis an excuse every man will plead, and no man can tell how to confute him.' Ignorance may, however, lessen a **sentence**.

illegitimate

The term used to describe a **child** born outside **marriage**. The Family Law Reform Act 1987 requires parents to treat legitimate and illegitimate children in virtually the same way as regards duties such as **maintenance**. Illegitimate children can inherit **property** under **wills** in the same way as legitimate children, unless the will specifies otherwise. The same applies if the parent dies without a will. Illegitimate children can get a short form of birth certificate which does not reveal their parents' names.

immigrant

Someone who enters a country other than his or her native country with the aim of living there permanently. UK immigration is controlled by the Immigration Acts of 1971 and 1988 and by a host of mind-numbingly complex rules made under them by various **Home Office** ministers. Anyone subject to this control needs permission to enter or remain in the UK. Permission may be for an indefinite or limited period and, if limited, there may be restrictions on their employment. Controls extend to all except citizens of Common Market countries and those who have a *right of abode* in the UK. The right of abode is limited to British citizens as defined by the British Nationality Act 1981 and to Commonwealth citizens who had the right of abode before the Act came into force.

impersonation

Pretending to be another individual. It is an **offence** to impersonate a voter, juror, police officer and certain public officials. It is **rape** to persuade a woman to have **sexual intercourse** by impersonating her husband, but few men are stupid enough to try this.

implied term; implied condition

A term or **condition** which is not stated in a **contract** but is implied by **law** to be present in it. For example, even if a contract does not say that the seller has the right to sell the goods or that they are of merchantable quality, the law will assume that those conditions were present. This enables the buyer to **sue** for damages if the implied condition is breached. A term may also be implied by custom of trade or a previous course of dealing. Some implied terms cannot by law be expressly excluded from the contract—see **unfair contract terms.**

in

A word used by **lawyers** in what many lay people consider odd constructions, for example: *I consider you have a case in negligence/defamation/breach of contract.* The lay person would probably say *for* instead, but lawyers tend to regard these things as categories of **claim** rather than pegs on which one might hang a claim. On the other hand, it would be better to say: *You have an action in tort,* as **tort** is an umbrella term for many different wrongs.

in camera

[Latin: in the chamber] A **court** hearing in private session, either in the **judge's** room behind the court or in a courtroom from which the public and press have been barred. Most

hearings are in *open court* unless the proceedings would offend public decency or prejudice public safety or national security.

incapax

[Latin: not capable] Someone who cannot look after his or her own affairs or instruct others to do so because of ill health.

See **age of responsibility; curator bonis; power of attorney.**

incest

The **offence** of **sexual intercourse** between a man and his daughter, grand-daughter, sister, half-sister, or mother; or between a woman of 16 or over and her grandfather, father, brother, half-brother or son, with her consent. In Scotland, sex between an uncle and niece, and an aunt and nephew, are also incest. It is not an offence if both **parties** are unaware they are related. **Prosecutions** are only brought with the agreement of the **Crown Prosecution Service.** Incest with a girl under 13 is punishable by **life imprisonment,** other offences by up to 7 years' jail. A girl under 16 cannot be prosecuted for incest.

incitement

The **offence** of persuading or trying to persuade someone to commit a **crime.** If the other individual does so, the inciter is also guilty of aiding and abetting it. Incitement includes threat, pressure or suggestion.

incompetent

In Scots law, an **action** is held to be incompetent if the **remedy** requested conflicts with a rule of **law** which applies to the **case.**

indecency

Conduct that an average individual would find shocking or revolting. This is left to a **jury** to decide.

See **obscene publications.**

indecent assault

An **assault** in circumstances that an ordinary individual would find shocking and revolting, punishable by up to 10 years in prison. Consent would prevent an indecent act being an assault but consent cannot be given by someone under 16. Touching someone's genitals without their consent would be an indecent assault. In Scots law, indecent assault is not a **crime** as such, being treated as an assault accompanied by indecency.

indecent exposure

The **offence** of exposing one's body beyond accepted standards of decency so that at least two people could have seen it, even if no-one was upset. A man exposing his genitals to a woman in order to insult her is **guilty** of indecent exposure and could be guilty of **indecent assault** if it was done threateningly or frighteningly.

indemnify

To fully protect against loss. If an **insurance policy** indemnifies you, it promises to restore you to your pre-loss position.

indictable offence

An **offence** triable before a **judge** and **jury,** such as **murder**. Lesser indictable offences such as **theft** may be tried on a summary basis, ie before a **magistrate**.

indictment

A document giving details of the **offence** for which someone is charged. It is read out to the **accused** at the trial.

industrial tribunal

A body set up under employment **law** to hear **cases** between employers and employees concerning terms of employment (including **unfair dismissal, redundancy, contracts** of employment, health and safety at work, equal pay and **maternity rights**), and between **trade unions** and their members. **Hearings** are more informal than in **court**. They are chaired by a **lawyer** of at least 7 years' standing, flanked by one employers' representative and one trade union representative. **Parties** can conduct their own cases or be represented at their own expense. **Legal aid** is not available. Tribunals sit at about 95 centres throughout the UK. The decision is by majority.

There is often a pre-hearing assessment where the tribunal considers written **statements** by the parties and may warn one side that it seems unlikely to succeed and could be ordered to pay the other side's **costs** if the case comes to a full **hearing**. Decisions can be appealed to the **Employment Appeal Tribunal.**

infanticide

A mother causing the death of a **child** less than 12 months' old while the mother's mind is disturbed because of the stress of childbirth or lactation. Infanticide is a lesser charge than **murder** and usually leads to a **sentence** of probation or conditional discharge. The **crime** was introduced in an Act of 1922 because juries were refusing to convict mothers of murder in such circumstances.

informer

People who provide information to the police about **crimes** committed by others.They may do this in return for a lighter **sentence** for their own part in the crime.

inheritance

The passing of **property** to someone on the death of its owner. This may occur as a result of a **will** or according to the **intestacy** rules.

inheritance tax

A tax payable on the value of someone's **estate** when he or she dies, plus the value of his or her gifts in the seven years before death. The rate of tax depends on the value of the estate and when the gifts were made. Other lifetime gifts will also be taxed, but at a different rate. Some gifts are exempt, for example those between husband and wife, to charities, and for public benefit.

inhibition

In Scots law, a form of **diligence** by which a **creditor** prevents a **debtor** from disposing of **heritage** or using it as **security**.

injunction

A **court** order instructing a **defendant** not to commit some act or, less often, to commit some act. As injunctions are often needed urgently, a special **hearing** of a court may grant a temporary (*interlocutory*) injunction before the full **case** is heard. The **plaintiff** must undertake to compensate the **defendant** if the main **action** goes against the plaintiff.

injuria

See **delict**.

injury

Actual harm to an individual or **property,** or a breach of legal duty which adversely affects someone, or an infringement of someone's right.

Inland Revenue

Money collected in the UK in taxes and stamp duties, and placed under the care of the Board of Inland Revenue. The day-to-day affairs of the Board are run by civil servants employed by HM Treasury. Individuals can appeal against their tax assessments to the General Commissioners for the district, who are lay people, or to a Special Commissioner, who is a full-time Treasury civil servant.

in loco parentis

[Latin: in the place of a parent] Often used to describe someone looking after **children** while their parents are elsewhere, such as a schoolteacher or relative. In **law** only the legal **guardian** or an individual having **parental responsibility** for the child can stand in loco parentis.

Inner House

In Scotland, part of the **Court of Session** which deals with **appeals** in **civil cases.**

Inns of Court

Voluntary societies with the exclusive right to confer the rank of **barrister** in England, Wales and Northern Ireland. In

England and Wales, four Inns have existed in London since the 14th century: Middle Temple, Inner Temple, Lincoln's Inn and Gray's Inn. These probably evolved from the hostels where early **law** practitioners lived together. In Northern Ireland the Inn of Court was established in Belfast in 1926. Inns are governed by benchers—**judges** and senior barristers who are co-opted, electing one of their number annually to be treasurer.

inquest

In English law, a **coroner's** inquiry into a death whose cause is unknown. Sometimes a **jury** will sit at an inquest. Possible **verdicts** include *unlawful killing, death by misadventure* (accident), **suicide,** *suicide aggravated by lack of care,* or an *open verdict* if it is unclear what happened. **Legal aid** is not available for the bereaved relatives of, say, an accident victim or someone who has died in **custody** to be represented at the hearing. Before the inquest, any legal representatives of a victim's family may not see documents in the coroner's possession which might shed light on what happened. This puts them at a disadvantage.

in re

[Latin: in the matter of] A way of referring to the name of a legal **case** or **law report**: *In re Smith v Jones (1939)*, or, abbreviated, *Re: Smith (1939)*. In abbreviated form it is used in the headings of letters: *Re: The hedge in your garden,* where the word is superfluous since the heading stands perfectly well without it.

insanity

A defect of the mind, arising from mental disease, which is severe enough to stop a **defendant** knowing what he or she did (or that it was wrong). Insanity is a **defence** if the individual can prove that at the time of the **offence** he or she was insane. Medical **evidence** can be brought but a **jury** will decide their **verdict** on the **facts**. People who commit **homicide** but are adjudged insane are usually detained in a special hospital. The usual verdict on someone adjudged insane is *not guilty by reason of insanity.*

insider dealing

The **offence** of dealing in company shares on a stock exchange while possessing confidential information gained from close connections with the company, whether as **director,** company secretary, employee or professional adviser. Before insider dealing was prohibited in 1985, it enriched those in the know—often to the detriment of outsiders who saw their share values evaporate overnight.

insolvency

The state of a company which is in financial ruin.

insolvency practitioner

Someone appointed to wind-up a company or sort out its **insolvency,** acting as, for example, **liquidator,** administrative receiver or **trustee in bankruptcy.** The Insolvency Act 1986 lays down qualifications for insolvency practitioners, one of which is membership of an approved professional body like the Insolvency Practitioners Association or the Institute of Chartered Accountants. It is an **offence** to act without qualifications.

instance

See **court of first instance.**

instant

1 In fusty **lawyers'** letters, the current month, as in *Thank you for your letter of the 15th instant.* More considerate lawyers look up to the heavens, work out the correct month from the conjunction of the planets, and write it in.

2 In **law reports,** *instant case* refers to the **case** being reported on—a useful way of distinguishing between that and other cases being discussed.

instruct

Tell or inform, as in *my client has instructed me that . . .* Hence, **solicitors** speak of *taking instructions* from their **clients.**

instrument

A piece of paper with writing or printing on it; a document. Long-winded **lawyers** will also use *instrument in writing, instrument of writing* and *written instrument.*

insufficient evidence

A **judge's** direction to a **jury** that there is not enough **evidence** to justify a **guilty verdict,** therefore they should acquit.

insurance policy

A document issued by an insurance company to specify the terms of a **contract** of insurance. In return for the payment of a premium, the company promises to pay a sum of money if a certain occurrence, like damage from fire, happens.

In life insurance (cheerily known in the trade as *life assurance,* since death is inevitable at some time) the company agrees to pay a sum to the insured's **estate** on the death of the insured or, if he or she reaches a certain age, to pay a sum to the insured. You can only insure the life of someone in whom you have an *insurable interest* such as yourself, your **marriage** partner, your **debtors** and **trustees.** This helps to prevent people insuring their enemies (or friends), then murdering them for the insurance money.

Under the Road Traffic Act 1972, the minimum motor insurance for drivers is **third party**. This covers liabilities to **third parties**—anyone you injure, including your passengers, while your car is on the public **highway,** being driven or not. (The *first party* is you, the *second party* is the insurer.)

Most events which are uncertain can be insured against provided the **person** seeking insurance has an insurable interest in the matter—this is one way of distinguishing insurance from gambling. So the organisers of the village fete can insure against the risk of rain ruining their big day.

The basis of insurance contracts is the doctrine of *utmost good faith* (Latin: *uberrimae fidei*). Anyone seeking insurance must therefore disclose all **facts** which an insurer might consider relevant when considering whether to accept the risk and on what terms. This causes problems, since few customers look at things in quite the same way as insurers. So it is wise to disclose everything that might be remotely relevant, and leave the company to sort it out.

Dissatisfied policyholders can take their case to the Insurance Ombudsman or **sue** in the **courts,** though many insurance policies contain a compulsory **arbitration** clause in case of disputes.

Traditionally the meaning of household and motor policies has been shrouded in legal jargon and minuscule print, but plain language policies have gradually become more fashionable since the early 1980s.

intellectual property

Rights in the product of intellectual effort. It includes **copyright** in published work, designs and **trade marks**, and **patents** granted to protect inventions.

intention

See **mens rea**.

inter alia

[Latin: among other things] Its rarer brother is *inter alios:* among other people.

interdict

In Scottish law, an **injunction**. Breach of an interdict is **contempt of court**. It can be granted if there are **reasonable** grounds for suspecting that some wrong or harm will occur to a **person** or **property**. It must specify the particular wrong which it aims to prevent. It cannot require the **defender** to take any specific course of action except to make good any harm or injury already done.

interest

In **land law,** a right in or over land.

interfering with witnesses

Trying to prevent **witnesses** from giving **evidence** or to influence the evidence they give. In some circumstances this may amount to **perverting the course of justice** or **contempt of court**.

interlocutor

In Scots law, any order of the **court**.

interlocutory proceedings

In English civil **litigation,** the preliminary stages between the start of the process and the trial. The stages include **pleading** and **disclosure of documents.** The aim is to set out the main issues to be tried and to prevent unexpected matters being raised at the trial.

See **surprise.**

International Court of Justice ('The World Court')

A **court** set up by the United Nations to hear **international law** disputes. Only nation states which accept its **jurisdiction** may be brought before the court. The court sits at The Hague, Netherlands, and is presided over by 15 **judges** who sit for 9-year terms.

international law

The **law** governing relationships between nation states, based principally on custom. There is no worldwide international law-making body, so the enforcement of international law by the International Court of Justice poses problems. The use of trade sanctions by an injured state may be worthless if the state is less powerful than the wrongdoer. The United Nations Security Council has a limited power to impose sanctions on behalf of member states. The success of sanctions depends on wide international co-operation, and even the most blackguard state can usually find a few friends to keep it supplied.

internment

Imprisonment without trial. It was used in Northern Ireland in the 1970s to curb terrorism but served only to win sympathy and recruits for the paramilitary groups.

interpretation

The judicial process of deciding the true meaning of a written document where there is doubt. Various rules of interpretation have been established to clarify **Acts of Parliament** and these apply equally to private documents like **deeds** and **wills.**

One rule is that a document must be interpreted as a whole; this helps to resolve any internal inconsistencies. There is therefore no need for all propositions, exceptions and provisos to be crammed into a single enormous sentence. The information can be split into separate short sentences with suitable linking words, or put into separate sections with clear headings.

Many documents open with an interpretation clause defining the meaning of certain words and phrases; this is established practice among **lawyers** and well understood by the **courts.** It can help to make documents more readable.

The Interpretation Act 1978 defines some common words and phrases and says that these apply in all other Acts unless shown otherwise. A court cannot resolve an ambiguity in a law by considering explanations of a proposed Act in a White Paper or ministerial statements during the Act's passage through **Parliament.**

See **eiusdem generis; golden rule; literal rule; sentence length.**

interrogation

The questioning of suspects by police. Suspects are not normally obliged to answer questions. Police duties and suspects' rights are governed by the Police and Criminal Evidence Act 1984 and the Codes made under it.

See **right to silence.**

intestacy

The situation where someone dies without having made a **will** or if the will is bad—for example, it may have been witnessed incorrectly. The individual is then said to have died intestate. *Partial intestacy* occurs when a will deals with only part of the **estate.** The intestacy rules, decided by **Act of Parliament,** govern how the estate will be administered, who benefits from it and what share they get. The estate normally goes to relatives.

in the event of
> Legalese for *if*.

intimidation
> The use of violence, threats etc. to compel someone to do or avoid doing something. Intimidation is not itself a **crime** but may form part of a crime. For example, intimidation which persuades someone to hand over money or goods may amount to **theft**. Someone intimidated into committing a crime may claim the **defence** of **duress**—'he said he'd kill me if I didn't steal it for him'.

intoxication
> Being **drunk** or under the influence of drugs. In a public place this is a **crime** and it may form part of a crime, such as drunken driving or being drunk and disorderly in a public place. It is an **offence** to supply alcohol to people under the age of 18 or to supply substances like glue or solvents which are likely to be inhaled to produce intoxication. A **contract** made with a drunkard may not be enforceable.
>
> See **drunkenness.**

invitation to treat
> An invitation to negotiate, such as a display of goods with a price tag attached or marked on them or an advertisement of items for sale. Every price tag is thus an invitation to haggle. In **contract law,** an invitation to treat is not the same as an offer and a customer cannot demand to have the goods at that price nor **sue** for breach of contract if they are refused him.

IOU
> Short for *I owe you*; a document signed by a **debtor** under this heading would probably be accepted as a valid admission of the debt to the holder of the document.

irregular marriage
> See **habit and repute.**

irritancy

In Scots law, the forfeiting of a right because of neglect or breach of some agreement.

itemized pay statement

A written statement which an employer must, by **law,** provide to an employee whenever wages or salary are paid to him or her. The statement must show: gross pay for the period; net pay; how the pay is calculated if different elements of it are calculated differently; and the amounts and reasons for deductions. An employee can go to an **industrial tribunal** if this is not given.

J

jactitation of marriage

An untrue statement that you are married to someone to whom you are not married. The individual affected used to be able to get an **injunction** preventing such claims, but this charming idiosyncrasy of English law was abolished in 1986.

joint and several

Legalese for *together and individually.* A **contract** in which two or more people are said to be *jointly and severally liable* means they can be sued together and as individuals for breaching their obligations. One of them, therefore, could be made to pay the full cost or bear the full loss. They are said to be **co-obligants.**

joint tenants

1 Two or more people who pay **rent** jointly under a letting agreement in England and Wales. To be regarded as joint tenants all their names should be on the rent book or rent agreement. A joint tenant may be able to take over the tenancy if the other joint tenant dies. See **assured tenancy; assured shorthold tenancy; regulated tenancy; secure tenancy.**

2 Confusingly, people who buy and own **land** or **property** together may also be called joint tenants. The term implies a 50/50 division of the purchase price or sale proceeds. The death of one of them would mean the survivor taking a 100% share. This differs from a *tenancy in common,* which divides the purchase price or sale proceeds in accordance with the contributions of the **parties.** Each then owns that specific share and can leave it by **will** to anyone they choose. A couple planning to buy a property together, whether they are married or not, should consider carefully which kind of agreement they want. If there is no agreement, joint tenancy will be assumed. Tenancy in common is unknown in Scotland.

See **cohabitation contracts; matrimonial home.**

judge

A public official with authority to adjudicate in civil and criminal **cases**. In England and Wales, judges are appointed by the Crown on the advice of the prime minister in the case of the **Court of Appeal** and the **House of Lords,** and on the advice of the **Lord Chancellor** in the case of High Court and **circuit judges.** Judges are appointed from the ranks of experienced **barristers,** though experienced **solicitors** may become circuit judges. Senior judges, apart from the Lord Chancellor (who is a government minister), can be removed only by both Houses of Parliament; this rule is meant to ensure judges' independence. Circuit judges can be removed by the Lord Chancellor for incapacity or misbehaviour.

Judges in the UK cannot be sued for their acts as judges (they can in the USA).

Judges in the UK are appointed by a secret system which depends heavily upon the views of the leading judges and barristers, who tend to favour people who are like themselves —according to the **Law Society.** As a result, relatively few women, black people and solicitors become judges. Only 4.5% of circuit judges, 5.6% of recorders and 6% of assistant recorders are women, yet women of relevant experience account for 11% of the practising profession. Of the 540 judges in 1990, 518 were men. The Lord Chancellor has said he hopes the influx of women lawyers since the 1970s will rectify the imbalance.

judge-made law

See **common law; precedent.**

judgment

A **court** decision or the line of reasoning which yielded the decision. By convention, the spelling of judgment in the legal sense has only one e; quite a saving in a field not noted for brevity.

judgment creditors

Creditors who can enforce a claim against a **debtor** (the *judgment debtor*) by quoting a **court** judgment in their favour.

See **oral examination.**

judgment summons

A **summons** requiring a **judgment debtor** to appear before a **court** and answer questions on **oath** about his or her means. If the debt concerns **maintenance** payments, taxes or national insurance contributions, and the judgment debtor could have paid but did not, the court can hand down a prison **sentence** suspended until instalments are paid.

judicial factor

In Scotland, an individual appointed by the court to manage the property of someone who cannot do so for themselves, eg a **child** or **incapax**.

judicial immunity

The exemption of **judges** and **magistrates** from being sued for **damages** arising from the duties of their office.

judicial review

In England and Wales, a legal way of using the **High Court** to reconsider decisions of lower **courts, tribunals** and administrative bodies like government departments. The High Court may make various orders, known as **prerogative orders: certiorari** (Latin: to be more informed), which brings the **case** into court and quashes the decision if it was wrong in **law** or outside the lower court's power to judge; **mandamus** (Latin: we command), which instructs a tribunal, public official etc to perform a duty it should have performed; and *prohibition,* which orders a tribunal or similar body not to perform an act outside its powers. The High Court may also award **damages** in these circumstances.

Applications for judicial review rose from 491 in 1980 to 2 129 in 1990.

judicial separation order

A rarely used alternative to **divorce** in which the **parties** cease to be obliged to live together but are not free to remarry. The petitioner (individual seeking the order) must prove one of the five grounds for breakdown of **marriage** (see **divorce**) but need not prove irretrievable breakdown of marriage. There is no three-year rule, so the petitioner can get a judicial separation when he or she could not get a divorce—useful for **battered wives** who want their separate status recognized to help prevent molestation by their husbands. In making a judicial separation order, the **court** has the same powers as regards **maintenance** and **children** as in divorce. Judicial separation can easily be converted to divorce by either party. This kind of order is attractive to people with religious objections to divorce.

junior barrister

A **barrister** who is not a **Queen's Counsel**. Junior does not necessarily imply youthfulness or inexperience.

jurat

A statement at the bottom of an **affidavit,** naming the **parties** and stating when, where and before whom it was signed.

jurisdiction

1 The authority of a **court** to hear a **case** or make an order.

2 The geographical area covered by a particular legal system. In the UK, the jurisdiction of England and Wales is separate from that of Scotland. There are many differences between English law (which covers England and Wales) and Scots law, though the two systems share most of the increasing volume of **statute law**. The **law** in Northern Ireland differs in minor respects from English law, for example in such matters as **abortion** and contraception. In the USA, individual states are separate jurisdictions and there may be considerable differences in law.

jurisprudence

The philosophy of **law**.

jurist

Someone knowledgeable about the science of **law,** or a writer on legal questions.

jury

A group of people, generally 12 (15 in Scotland), who try the **facts** in a criminal **case** in the **Crown Court** or, more rarely, in a **civil case** or **inquest**. In England and Wales jurors (members of the jury) are chosen at random from the electoral roll and must be aged between 18 and 65. Certain people cannot serve on a jury—for example, members of the judiciary, the clergy and the mentally ill—or may be excused if they are MPs or doctors. People with certain kinds of criminal convictions are also disqualified. In practice, others are often excused if they offer compelling reasons—sole traders, for instance, whose business would be severely hit by a prolonged period of jury service. But the danger of widespread avoidance of jury service is that the principle of a random jury is eroded.

If too few jurors have been summoned, the **court** can bring in an eligible individual off the street, a process called *praying the tails*. The unfortunate is called a *talesman*.

There has been pressure to stop jury trial in certain cases like complicated fraud where the issues are difficult to follow. In Northern Ireland, some serious crimes are tried without a jury because of **intimidation** of jurors: the **Diplock courts.**

Jurors may take notes and ask questions during a trial if they wish to clarify a point. Jury-room discussions must not be reported. In England and Wales, a majority **verdict** of 10–2 is permitted if jurors cannot reach a unanimous verdict.

Jurors must recite a measure of quaint English before taking part in a criminal trial, promising: 'I will faithfully try the several issues joined between our sovereign lady the Queen and the prisoner at the Bar, and give a true verdict according to the evidence.'

It is an **offence,** known as *embracery,* to seek to influence a jury by bribery or threats.

Jury trial is a British invention which began in the early 13th century to replace trial by the ordeals of fire and water, in which guilt or innocence was decided by ritual tests overseen by parish priests. It took many centuries, however, before juries felt secure enough to give verdicts opposite to those expected by the **judges.** Only since 1972 have people who do not own **property** been able to serve on a jury.

jury box

An enclosure where the **jury** sit in **court**.

jury challenge

The right of **prosecution** and **defence** to challenge the make-up of the **jury** before it is sworn in. A challenge may be to the whole panel, alleging that the jury was summoned in a biased way, or, more commonly, to individual jurors. The prosecution can challenge without giving a reason and the juror will automatically be stood down. The defence must give reasons for a challenge and the **judge** decides whether the individual will stay or be stood down.

jury point

Lawyers describe as a good jury point one that lacks any real relevance or force but has a superficial attraction to **jury** members who lack the training or experience to spot its defects.

jury vetting

The checking by police and the **Special Branch** of potential jurors' political sympathies and previous behaviour. Although the police always check whether potential jurors have a criminal record, which usually disqualifies them, jury vetting refers to a wider investigation than illegal conduct. It tends to be used in trials involving terrorism or criminal gangs. Police and the Special Branch trawl their files for conduct which they consider abnormal, such as attending demonstrations or being involved in squatting. Information is passed to the **prosecution** who will challenge that juror and have him or her removed from the **case**.

Justice

A law reform society which conducts research into ways of improving the administration of the **law** and publishes reports on this. The society takes a special interest in individual **cases** of injustice, which may signpost the need for reform.

justice

1 An ideal that the **law** seeks to uphold in the setting right of wrongs and the protection of rights and freedoms. Disraeli described justice as 'truth in action.'

2 Short for **justice of the peace.**

justice of the peace (JP)

See **magistrate.**

juvenile court

In England and Wales, a **magistrates' court** which deals with **offences** committed by young people (those aged under 18) and other matters relating to such **children.** The **court** consists of three **magistrates** from a special panel; one must be a woman. The proceedings are closed to the public. The names of the children concerned must not be published without special leave. The court tends to be more informal than others. A young offender charged with an adult may have to appear in an adult court and then appear again before the juvenile court for trial and sentence. From October 1992, the juvenile court becomes the **youth court.**

K

keeping the peace

Behaving in a way that does not disturb public order. **Magistrates courts** have wide powers to bind over people to keep the peace or require them to pay money into **court** on any future **breach of the peace.** If a **defendant** refuses these sanctions, he or she can be imprisoned though no criminal **offence** has been committed.

kerb crawling

The **offence** committed by a man of soliciting a woman for prostitution from a motor vehicle in a street or public place. Proof is difficult since the kerb crawling must normally be persistent and blatant for a **court** to convict. Persistence means several single invitations to one individual or several invitations to different people. Rather than prosecute, police may prefer to write to persistent offenders, hint that their vehicles have been seen driving up and down a street several times, and suggest they buy a map.

kidnap

Taking someone away without their consent using force, threats or **fraud.** A man may be **guilty** of kidnapping his wife. The maximum penalty is **life imprisonment.**

kin

Blood relatives.

King's Counsel

See **barrister.**

knock-for-knock

An agreement between insurance companies to pay claims made by their own customer and so avoid the expense of claiming from each other.

L

laches

/ˈlætʃɪz/

Unreasonable delay in enforcing or pursuing a legal right. A **court** will not help someone who, in full knowledge of the **facts,** takes too long to bring an **action,** for example to set aside an agreement obtained by **deception**.

land

Parts of the surface of the earth which can be owned. In **law, land** also includes the buildings upon it, the subsoil below it and the airspace above it (though aircraft have the right to overfly at a **reasonable** height). Sir Edward Coke's ancient definition put it this way: 'Land in the legal signification comprehendeth any ground, soil or earth whatsoever, as meadows, pastures, woods, moors, waters, marshes, furzes and heath . . . It legally includeth also all castles, houses and other buildings.'

See **common law; fixtures.**

land charge

A legal **interest** in **land,** such as a **mortgage, restrictive covenant** or **easement,** which imposes an obligation on the landowner in favour of someone else. If registered with the **Land Registry,** the land charge binds future purchasers of the land.

landlord

A **person** who grants a **lease** or tenancy, also known as a **lessor.** The landlord need not be the owner and may be a **tenant.** There are laws governing what a landlord can charge for services such as electricity and how certain landlords, such as **housing associations,** must consult with their tenants. The person receiving the rent must reveal the landlord's name on the tenant's request.

land registration

A procedure in which ownership of **land** is officially registered. Registration simplifies the transfer of land between sellers and buyers.

See **Land Registry; Land Registry of Scotland; Sasines, Register of.**

Land Registry (HM Land Registry)

The public body which maintains registers on the ownership of **land** in England and Wales. Its main register contains ownership details of 13 million houses and other buildings and plots of land. Registration is not compulsory in all areas, making it impossible to discover who owns most of the land. The register is open to the public. Anyone may therefore find out who owns a registered **property,** whether it is mortgaged and to which lender, and what **restrictive covenants** may affect it. Information can usually be had by post for an £18 fee.

A land certificate (charge certificate if the land is mortgaged) issued by the registry provides evidence of ownership, known as **title.** The certificate is in three parts:

1 the property register which gives a plan of the land, describes the land and states any **rights of way** over adjoining land;

2 the proprietorship register which names the owners and says what kind of title they hold in it;

3 the charges register which states any **land charges.**

The land certificate takes the place of traditional *title deeds.* Errors by the registry, for example in registering the same land in the names of two separate **parties,** are subject to **compensation** for the value of the land and legal fees to the aggrieved party.

See **Land Registry of Scotland; Sasines, Register of.**

Land Registry of Scotland

A gradually developing register of **land** ownership in Scotland. It keeps records in a similar way to the **Land Registry.** When the Land Registry of Scotland's records are complete, the **Register of Sasines** will close.

Lands Tribunal

A public body which hears **compensation** disputes in cases of compulsory purchase by government, **local authorities** etc.

last will and testament

A phrase which, stripped of redundant words, means merely **will**. This is because a will is a **testament** and a *last will* is the same as a will, since no-one can be sure whether another later will exists. Will was Old English, testament was its Latin equivalent. Will has the advantage of being readily understood by the will-maker and **witnesses**.

law

1 Specifically, a rule of conduct laid down by a controlling authority.

2 Generally, the whole body of such rules, recognized and enforced by society in the **courts.** Laws are made by the body which has the constitutional authority to make them—in the UK, Parliament. But there is also the **common law,** an amalgam of **natural justice** and previous **court** decisions which interpret the law and in some ways create new law.

In states with a written constitution, such as the USA, the Supreme Court may have the power to overturn particular laws as unconstitutional, ie inconsistent with the fundamentals of society.

The word is Old English, having prevailed over the Latin *lex* and *ius*.

See **delegated legislation.**

law centre

A body staffed by salaried **lawyers** and advice workers which provides legal services to poor people in their area, although there is no formal means test. Law centres specialize in work which mainstream **solicitors** find unattractive, perhaps because it is too complicated or badly paid, like legally aided **cases** on immigration, tenancies and juvenile **crime.** They also take up cases on behalf of large groups, such as council **tenants** trying to force a **local authority** to do repairs. Law centres must not compete with mainstream solicitors on certain types of case—for example, **divorce,** conveyancing and large personal injury cases. There are only about 50 law centres throughout England and Wales. Funding is a serious problem for them, especially as their work may bring them into conflict with the organizations who fund them, such as local authorities.

Law Commission

A body which examines the **law** and recommends reforms and the repeal of outdated laws and anomalies. Members are **judges, barristers, solicitors** and academics appointed by the **Lord Chancellor.** It is staffed by civil servants from the Lord Chancellor's Department. The commission has some influence but little reforming zeal and no power. Most of its reports moulder ignored on Whitehall shelves. Theoretically it is independent of government. Scotland has its own Law Commission.

law of the sea

The rules of **international law** embodied in the United Nations Convention on the Law of the Sea (1982). *Internal waters* include ports, rivers, lakes and canals. *Territorial waters* include the width of sea adjacent to a coastal state, traditionally 3 miles, which legally belongs to that state. Foreign ships have a right of innocent passage through territorial waters; this does not extend to foreign aircraft in the air space above the waters. Outside the territorial waters are the *high seas* which may be freely used by all ships. English **courts** have **jurisdiction** over **offences** committed by anyone anywhere in the world on board a British ship or a British-controlled aircraft in flight. Many states claim exclusive economic zones extending beyond territorial waters; for example, exclusive fishery rights extending for 200 miles.

law reports

Records of important **court** decisions which show the **barristers'** line of argument and the **judges'** reasoning. As year books, law reports appeared as early as the reign of Edward I. Reports are useful because they reveal **precedents** which a barrister may try to persuade the court to follow. The courts rely heavily on law reports in developing the **law,** so they are treated as a source of law in themselves. Modern law reports are revised by judges before issue.

The reference to a law report is abbreviated. Thus, for example, 'Tucker v Farm and General Investment Trust Ltd [1966] 2 All ER 508, CA' represents: a case reported in 1966; recorded in the second volume of the All England Law Reports; starting on page 508; and heard in the **Court of Appeal.** Libraries in major cities carry copies of law reports. Current cases of importance are reported in the broadsheet daily newspapers and, if signed by a barrister, may be cited in court.

Reports of important decisions in Scots law are published in Session Cases and the Scots Law Times.

Law Society

The professional body for **solicitors** in England and Wales; separate societies exist in Scotland and in Northern Ireland. It furthers the interests of solicitors, regulates their conduct and organizes examinations, education and training through the College of Law. It issues annual practising certificates without which solicitors may not practise.

See **Solicitors Complaints Bureau.**

lawyer

One who practises or is qualified in **law,** either as a **solicitor** or **barrister.**

Names for lawyers include *mouthpiece, lip, legal beagle,* and, from 20th-century American, *legal eagle.* Many other names for lawyers are uncomplimentary, continuing an ancient tradition of vilifying the profession which began in St Luke's Gospel with the denunciation: 'Woe unto you, lawyers! for ye have taken away the key of knowledge: ye entered not in yourselves, and them that were entering in ye hindered.'

In the USA the avocet, a bird of the shoreline, is called a lawyer on account of its 'perpetual clamour and flippancy of tongue', while another bird is also known as a lawyer 'on account of its long bill'. One fish is called a *lake-lawyer* because of its 'ferocious looks and voracious habits'. *Shyster,* possibly from the German *scheisse* (excrement) is given as 'lawyer' in American dictionaries from the 1840s. *Ambulance chaser* has been a vogue term in the USA since the advent of the railroads, apparently in reference to the prompt arrival at accidents of lawyers drumming up trade.

Lawyer-abuse has continued for centuries. A Spanish colonist in North America wrote to his king in 1513: 'One thing I supplicate your majesty: that you will give orders, under a great penalty, that no bachelors of law should be allowed to come here; for not only are they bad themselves, but they also make and contrive a thousand iniquities.' In 16th century England, Thomas More's Utopia daydreamed of a lawyerless world: 'They have no lawyers among them, for they consider them as a sort of people whose profession it is to disguise matters.' In the 18th century, Jonathan Swift, in Gulliver's Travels, joined distaste for lawyers with that of their language: 'I said there was a Society of Men among us, bred up from their Youth in the Art of proving by Words multiplied for the purpose, that White is Black and Black is White, according as they are paid. To this Society all the rest of the People are Slaves.'

In the 19th century Jeremy Bentham waged war on lawyers and their habits of language. He described lawyers as 'the harpies of the law' who understood 'the art of poisoning language in order to fleece their clients.' He spoke of lawyers' language as the 'Principle of Jargon and Jargonisation', 'excrementitious matter' and 'literary garbage'. In this, he said, the **judges** were senior partners, delighting in the complexity of the system and feeling 'a degree of awkwardness where a decision is to be given upon the merits [of the **case**].'

Burdened by so much calumny, it is a wonder that modern lawyers ever manage to do a conscientious and effective job for their **clients.**

See **barrister; solicitor.**

lay member

Someone who is not legally qualified but who sits on a judicial **tribunal** or acts as an observer.

laying an information

Putting a written or spoken **statement** before a **magistrate** alleging that a criminal **offence** has been committed. Anyone can do this but normally the police do. It is the first step in getting a **summons** or **arrest warrant** issued.

leader

The senior of two **barristers** appearing in **court** for the same **person**; known in Scotland as *senior counsel.*

leading case

A **case** where the decision establishes an important point of **law**.

leading question

Either a question asked of a **witness** in a way that suggests the answer: *You were in the house that night, weren't you?* or that assumes the truth of some disputed **fact**. Leading questions are permitted during **cross-examination** but not **examination-in-chief**.

lease

A **contract** in which the **landlord** (**lessor**) grants the **tenant** (**lessee**) the right to occupy the **property** exclusively for an agreed time, in return for **rent**. The length of time may be fixed (eg 10 years) or periodic (eg weekly). The terms of the lease state the obligations on both sides.

leasehold

A way of owning **land** (this includes the buildings on it), under a **lease**. Houses or flats can be owned leasehold or **freehold**. The leaseholder of a house may have to pay a small **ground rent** to the freeholder, but usually has the right to buy the freehold. The leaseholder of a flat will normally have to pay a service charge for the upkeep of common facilities.

leave

Permission that a **court** may give. For example the **Court of Appeal** may give or refuse leave to **appeal** to the **House of Lords**.

legacy

The gift of **personal property** by **will**. *Legatee* means someone to whom the gift is given.

Legal aid

A scheme which provides people with advice and assistance from **solicitors,** and aid with **representation** at every stage of civil and criminal trial, even up to **appeal**. The money comes from public funds but assisted people may also have to make contributions, depending on their means.

In a **civil case,** some **costs** may be recovered also from the opposing **party** if the legally aided individual wins, and from the value of, for example, **property** recovered by the **action**. The latter is called the *Statutory Charge.*

The declared aim of the scheme is to put assisted people on the same footing as those paying for their own **lawyer**. In urgent **cases** it may be possible to get *emergency legal aid*. In 1990–91 the total cost of legal aid was over £500 million, a 20% increase on the previous year.

Legal aid comes in several types:

1 Legal advice and assistance from a solicitor which includes advice on most legal problems. This is also known as the *Green Form Scheme.*

2 Civil legal aid if your civil case is more complex and needs to go to **court.**

3 Criminal legal aid if you are accused of a criminal **offence**. The court decides whether you qualify for this.

If you are not sure whether you qualify for legal aid, you can ask a solicitor who does legal aid work for a £5 *fixed fee interview.* This gives you half an hour's advice, and in practice many solicitors don't charge anything for it.

At 1991 figures, you will get legal advice and assistance if your net disposable income is less than £135 a week and your savings less than £935.

To get free civil legal aid, your net disposable income must be less than £2 645 a year (this is the figure after deduction of tax, national insurance contributions, pension plan premiums, maintenance payments, housing costs and travel-to-work costs). Up to a disposable income of £6350 you get legal aid but make a contribution based on a sliding scale related to income.

There is also a savings means test. For all fees to be met by legal aid, you must have less than £3000 (apart from the value of your home). Again there is a sliding scale up to a cut-off of £6310. If you are on income support, you get civil legal aid regardless of your savings. To get civil legal aid you must show that you have a legal case which could be proved and that bringing the case is **reasonable** and not a waste of public funds.

At many **magistrates' courts** there is a **duty solicitor** to give free legal advice and **representation** on criminal cases on your first appearance. There is no means test. The same applies if the police question you about an **offence,** whether they **arrest** you or not.

In Scotland, free legal aid for the poor began in 1424 under an Act which remained in place until 1949.

See **legal expenses insurance.**

legalese

A mildly derogatory term for the language customarily used by **lawyers** in their speech, letters and other documents. Legalese can be divided into two categories:

1 Unnecessary **legal flavouring**: words like hereof, **thereof** and **whereof,** which lack any special meaning and can be omitted or replaced by modern English.

2 Useful **terms of art**: technical legal words and phrases which have recognized meanings among lawyers, like **mandamus, mens rea, mistake, negligence.**

Legalese is sometimes used to describe other features of traditional legal writing, such as long sentences.

See **sentence length.**

legal executive

Someone who is not a **solicitor** but who does some of the solicitor's work, such as taking **statements** from **witnesses** and handling routine **divorce,** conveyancing and **probate** work. Legal executives may be more competent in their own area of expertise than a solicitor but they usually work under the supervision of a solicitor. They belong to the Institute of Legal Executives, having qualified by passing the Institute's exams and serving a period of apprenticeship.

legal expenses insurance

A way of insuring against the cost of legal proceedings. There are two types: an addition to your usual home contents or car insurance cover; and a separate policy, which is more costly. The kind of cover varies widely so it is important to read the policy carefully and compare it with others. Some policies only cover consumer complaints, accidents and employment disputes. Most exclude **divorce** and disputes arising from the construction or extension of buildings.

Restrictions on **legal aid** and the high cost of **litigation** have made these policies more attractive, but if you are covered by legal expenses insurance you cannot get legal aid.

legal fiction

Something which the **law** regards as true even though everyone knows it isn't, for example that all citizens know every word of the law.

legal flavouring

See **legalese.**

legal memory

The period from the start of the reign of Richard I, 1189. *Time immemorial* is the time before that.

See **living memory.**

legal personality

See **limited liability company; person.**

Legal Services Ombudsman

An official appointed by the government under the Courts and Legal Services Act 1990 to investigate how professional bodies for **solicitors, barristers** and **licensed conveyancers** handle complaints against their members. He or she can order the different complaint machineries to improve their practices and to pay **compensation** if they botch a complaint. The ombudsman can also order individual practitioners to pay compensation. Normally the ombudsman can only take up a complaint from a **client** if it has been finished with by the professional body or if it has been ruled on by a **court** or disciplinary **tribunal.** The ombudsman cannot deal with a complaint about a barrister's handling of a **case** in court.

legal year

The period of the four court sittings in the Supreme Court in any year. The sittings are Michaelmas, Hilary, Easter and Trinity. The gaps are the four vacations: Long, Christmas, Easter and Whitsun. The Long Vacation runs from 1 July to 30 September; only urgent business is done then.

legislation

Acts of Parliament and **laws** made under powers given by Acts of Parliament.

See **common law; community law; delegated legislation.**

legislature

The institution recognized as having power to make **laws.** In the UK this means the Queen-in-Parliament, comprising the monarch (whose role is purely formal), the **House of Lords,** the **House of Commons,** and bodies empowered to make **delegated legislation.**

legitimacy

The legal status of a **child** born to parents who were married to each other at the time of conception or birth. In practice there is now little legal difference between legitimate and **illegitimate** children. When the mother is married, children of the marriage are assumed to be offspring of the mother's husband, though this can be refuted by **evidence** of the father's absence or impotence or by blood-testing or **DNA testing**. A child may be legitimated in various ways, for example by its parents marrying after birth.

lesion

In Scots law, injury, loss or detriment.

lessee

See **tenant**.

lessor

See **landlord**.

letters of administration

A **court's** authority to someone to act as administrator of a **deceased's estate** if he or she died without making a valid **will**.

liable relative

See **maintenance**.

libel

[From Latin *libellus*: a little book] **Defamation** of a living **person** (which includes a company or **local authority**) or group of people by means of published writing, pictures or broadcast statements, so as to injure their reputation or degrade them in the opinion of others. A rule of thumb to decide whether something is libellous is to ask 'Is it a false statement that discredits someone?'

For your reputation to be injured, you must have a reputation to lose. If you are a convicted murderer, newspapers can get away with saying almost anything damaging about you. Libel is usually a **civil court** matter, but a criminal libel case is possible if the defamation could provoke a **breach of the peace**.

Normally only the rich and those certain of success can afford to **sue** for civil libel, as the **case** must be heard in the higher, more expensive **courts**. A common alternative to **litigation** is to persuade the publisher to print a prominent agreed apology even if this lacks the force of the original story. In practice most cases are settled out of court. **Legal aid** is not available to bring or defend libel proceedings.

Defences to a libel **action** may rely on *justification* (the statement was true), *fair comment* (I wrote it in the public interest, in good faith and without malice), and *privilege* (I'm only repeating what was said in court or **Parliament**).

A letter sent to an individual cannot normally be libellous unless it is published in some way. Publication might, however, include a secretary opening and reading the letter. Libel is one of the few civil claims tried by **jury**. When the jury finds in favour of the **plaintiff** it also decides on the amount of **damages,** without having to give a reason. Some juries appear to lose their heads at this stage, awarding sums which are vastly more than those to people who have been maimed in accidents arising from **negligence**. Lord Aldington won £1.5 million, Jeffrey Archer £500 000, Koo Stark £300 000, a fisherman accused of cheating in an angling competition £150 000.

Scots law speaks of **defamation,** not libel; it means the publication of a false statement to someone's discredit.

Liberty

An independent and non-party-political pressure group which aims to defend and extend civil liberties in the UK. Liberty pursues **test cases** in the **courts** and produces reports which monitor and analyse civil liberty issues. Its priorities include **privacy,** equal rights for women, political vetting of job applicants and jurors, policing and prisoners' rights.

licence

1 Authority to do something that is otherwise unlawful, for example to sell intoxicating liquor.

2 Permission to enter or occupy **land,** usually without giving a right to its exclusive possession.

licensed conveyancer

See **conveyancing.**

licensee

See **licence; licensed premises**.

licensed premises

Premises which have a **justices' licence** to sell intoxicating liquor for drinking on or off the premises (*an on-licence*) or off the premises only (*an off-licence*).

lie down

In police slang, a short-term remand in a police station: 'The **magistrate** gave him a 3-day lie down.' It is welcomed by the police as it allows them to continue their enquiries more easily and avoids having to transport the suspect to a distant **remand** centre.

lien

/'liːən/

A **creditor's** right to hold the **property** of a **debtor** until the debt is paid. For example, a garage might have a lien over a car being repaired.

life insurance

See **insurance**.

life imprisonment

A **sentence** involving imprisonment for the rest of someone's life. In the UK it is the only sentence for **murder,** and the maximum for **manslaughter, rape** and **arson**. Prisoners rarely serve life, being released on **licence** by the Home Secretary on the advice of the Parole Board after consultation with the **Lord Chief Justice** and, if possible, the trial **judge**. When passing this sentence, the judge may recommend a minimum term of imprisonment, though this is not binding.

life interest

An **interest** in **property** which lasts during the lifetime of the individual to whom it is given (*I give this field to Jones during his life*) or to someone else (*I give this house to Jones while his wife is alive*).

liferent

In Scots law, a right to possess and use **property** during one's life without destroying or damaging it, ie the liferenter must leave it substantially intact.

lifting the veil

A rare device used by the **courts** which allows them to ignore the veil of incorporation which separates a **limited liability company** (or some other **corporation**) from the main people who run it. Unmasking enables **frauds** to be more easily pinned on those who perpetrate them.

light or prospect

In Scots law, a restriction on owners of **servient tenements** which could take the form of any or all of the following **servitudes:**

1 of not building: owners must not build on their own **land;**

2 of not raising higher: they must not raise buildings beyond a certain height;

3 of not harming the light: they must not build so as to cut off the **dominant tenement's** light or view.

These are often known by their respective Latin names: *non aedificandi; altius non tollendi* and *non officiendi luminibus.*

limitation of actions

Rules which require civil **actions** to be brought within specific time limits. In England and Wales, for **tort** and simple **contract,** the period is six years from the event which gives rise to the action, though for personal injury and death it is three years. These periods may be extended in some circumstances. In **criminal law, summary offences** are normally subject to a 6-month time limit.

limited liability company (limited company)

A **corporation** registered under the Companies Act, each shareholder's liability being limited by the number of shares he or she has taken. If the company is private its name must end with *Limited* or *Ltd.* If its shares are on sale to the public, the name must end with *public limited company* or *plc.* (Other countries' equivalents include Inc, SA, and NV.)

The purpose of limited liability is to reduce the **directors'** level of risk. One company formation specialist explains the concept of separate **legal personality** in its prospectus: 'The company . . . has a completely separate legal existence . . . a limited company can help you in the instance of business failure . . . the directors have no personal liability in relation to a limited company.' There are other advantages, it says: 'With good tax planning . . . it is possible for your accountant to allay a considerable amount of tax, and, in most cases, negate corporation tax completely.' In Spanish the term for legal liability translates as 'The Society of the Faceless Ones.'

liquidator

Normally, a qualified **insolvency practitioner** who conducts the winding-up of a company. He or she is usually an accountant or **lawyer** with several years' relevant experience and an insolvency licence. The liquidator gets in the money that the company is owed and pays its debts, having given notice to **creditors** inviting them to send in their claims with sufficient proof. If the assets equal or exceed the debts, the creditors are paid in full. If not, the creditors merely receive a dividend, from a few pence in the £ to the bulk of the amount owed. The liquidator reports to the Department of Trade and Industry on the conduct of all **directors** of the liquidated company in the 3 years before the liquidation. This report may form the basis of disqualification of the directors from holding a similar position for a number of years. About 1 000 people were disbarred from 1986–91, usually for trading while the company was insolvent. Liquidation allows creditors to claim VAT bad debt relief for any VAT owed by the insolvent company.

See **winding-up order**.

listed building

A building designated of special architectural or historic interest on a list compiled or approved by the Department of the Environment. Local planning authority consent is needed for demolition or alteration. The list grades the buildings according to their importance.

literal rule

A rule used when interpreting **Acts of Parliament**. It says that the words in an Act must be applied strictly and literally, taking a narrow view of their meaning. It has been described as 'a rule against using intelligence in understanding language.'

See **interpretation; golden rule.**

litigant

A **party** to a **civil case**. Litigants may pay a **solicitor** or **barrister** to represent them in **court** and, if successful, will usually win back their **costs**. Litigants may choose to represent themselves in court (they are then known as *litigants-in-person*). If they win, they can usually reclaim their own costs. A *vexatious litigant* takes legal action merely to annoy an opponent and a court can throw out the action accordingly. Being a litigant can be expensive and many solicitors do their best to persuade their **clients** to settle out of court. A famous cartoon entitled 'litigation' portrays a farmer pulling at the horns of a cow while another pulls the tail. Crouched beneath the beast, a barrister milks the cow.

litigation

Legal **action.**

living memory

Time past which people alive today can personally remember. In disputes about ancient **rights of way** etc, old people may be called upon to testify whether they remember a path being used freely when they were **children.**

living on immoral earnings

An **offence** committed by a man who uses money obtained directly from female prostitution or from supplying services associated with it, such as advertising a prostitute's availability or driving clients to her place of work. It is also an offence for a man or woman to live off male prostitution. A **landlord** who rents accommodation to prostitutes does not commit the offence unless the **rent** is set higher because of the trade.

local authority

The body of councillors elected by the people of a local government area to run local government. In England and Wales, the top two tiers of **local authority** are county councils and district councils. In England the third tier is the parish council, in Wales the community council. Councillors are elected for 4 years.

lodger

Someone who lives in part of a **property** in return for **rent,** the property being under the owner's close control. The lodger usually has a **licence** not a tenancy.

London Gazette

A government journal for the publication of official notices like proclamations, windings up and receivership orders. In Scotland the Edinburgh Gazette does a similar job.

long tenancy

A fixed-term tenancy of more than 21 years.

Lord Advocate

A senior member of the Scottish **Bar** who is the Crown's chief **law** officer in Scotland, equivalent to the **Attorney General** in England. He or she has final responsibility for criminal **prosecutions** in Scotland and drafts **legislation** for Scotland. Normally he or she resigns office when there is a change of government.

Lord Chancellor

The head of the judiciary in England and Wales and of Scotland, a member of the cabinet and the individual who presides over the **House of Lords.** The Lord Chancellor may appoint and dismiss **magistrates** and **circuit judges.** As a prominent holder of positions in all three branches of government, the Lord Chancellor is a clear exception to the doctrine of the separation of the judiciary from the government of the day.

See **separation of powers**.

Lord Chief Justice (LCJ)

The head of the Queen's Bench Division of the **High Court**; also the president of the Criminal Division of the **Court of Appeal**. He or she is second to the **Lord Chancellor** in the legal hierarchy.

Lord Justice of Appeal (LJ)

Lord Justice of Appeal, an ordinary **judge** of the **Court of Appeal**.

Lord Ordinary

In Scotland, a **judge** of the **Court of Session** who sits in the Outer House.

loss of amenity

Partial or complete loss of a **plaintiff's** mental or physical capacity, arising from personal injury. In a claim for **damages,** the plaintiff can seek money for **loss of amenity** as well as pain and suffering, loss of earnings etc. A **court** would take account of loss of ability to carry on previously enjoyed pastimes, but someone whose hobby had been stamp collecting could not claim for being unable to take up hang gliding.

lottery

A game of chance, or a distribution of prizes or money by chance, without any choice or skill. There are strict controls on their use and they are usually illegal unless they are: on behalf of registered charities or sports; restricted to private club members; local lotteries approved by a **local authority;** or small lotteries taking place as part of an entertainment like a dance.

lump-sum award

The usual form in which **damages** are awarded by a **court**. Provisional **awards** may be given as an alternative if the victim's condition has not stabilized.

See **structured settlement**.

M

magistrate

A judicial appointment in England and Wales, also known as a **Justice of the Peace (JP)**. Magistrates are appointed and may be removed by the **Lord Chancellor**. Their main role is to preside in the **magistrates' courts,** administering immediate (*summary*) **justice** in most cases but committing the most serious **cases** for trial elsewhere.

Magistrates deal with about 95% of criminal cases; they are thus the mainstay of the criminal justice system. They are unpaid, part-time and amateur, though most now receive some training. Magistrates are chosen in secret on the advice of a secret advisory committee in each area; the names of committee members will be revealed from 1992 onwards. Anyone can apply to be a magistrate and occasionally there are public advertisements for them. Various groups cannot become magistrates, among them the police, traffic wardens, members of the armed forces and people with convictions for serious **offences**. Each magistrate exercises powers in a particular area only, known as a *commission area,* and sits with at least one colleague. Magistrates are unlikely to hold a legal qualification; they consider the **facts** of the case only, like a **jury,** and take advice on points of **law** from a legally qualified **clerk of the court.**

See **stipendiary magistrate.**

magistrates' court

A **court** where **magistrates** preside. All criminal prosecutions start here. By custom and by its use in **Acts of Parliament** (eg, the Magistrates' Courts Act 1980) there should always be an apostrophe after the s in magistrates' court, irritating though this may be.

Magna Carta

A charter signed by King John in 1215 under compulsion from the barons who had rebelled against him; it guaranteed the privileges of the barons and the church. Magna Carta proclaimed **justice** for all, but had little effect on the lives of most people. They remained at the mercy of a dubious system of justice imposed and enforced by the barons and the church. In modern law Magna Carta has no significance as most of its provisions have been repealed.

maintenance

Provision of food, clothing and other essentials of life. In **law,** a husband must maintain his wife, and vice versa, and they must maintain their **children** whether legitimate or not. Refusal to maintain can sometimes be a criminal **offence**. Single mothers who claim state benefits for children must reveal the identity of the father otherwise they risk losing benefit; the Department of Social Security can then pursue the father for maintenance. After **divorce,** a **court** may order one of the partners to provide maintenance for the other (and for any children)—the usual term for this is *financial provision* or, in Scotland, *periodical allowance.*

See **liable relative**.

majority

The age of 18 years. Someone becoming 18 is said to have *reached their majority.*

See **minority**.

making off without payment

The **offence** of leaving a taxi, restaurant etc without paying for goods or services received in order to avoid payment, where on-the-spot payment is expected.

malfeasance

An unlawful act.

malice aforethought

See **mens rea**.

malicious prosecution

Taking legal proceedings without **reasonable** cause. A police officer who fabricated **evidence** and used it in a **prosecution** could be sued for malicious prosecution by the victim.

mandamus

See **judicial review**.

mandate

Authority from one **person** to another to take some action. A customer's instruction to a bank to pay direct debits from an account is a kind of mandate.

mandatory

Required by **law,** compulsory.

man of skill

In Scots law, an expert (male or female) who provides a report to the **court** on some question which arises in a **case**.

man of straw

Someone who is not worth suing because he or she lacks the resources to pay.

manslaughter

Unlawful **homicide** which does not amount to **murder**. If there is an intention to cause death but, for example, there is a mitigating factor like **provocation, diminished responsibility** or a **suicide** pact, this is *voluntary manslaughter*. If there is no intention to cause death but, for example, there is grossly negligent behaviour which resulted in death, this is *involuntary manslaughter*.

The word is Old English and was once the equivalent of the Latin-based homicide (man-killing).

See **culpable homicide; reckless driving.**

Mareva injunction

In England and Wales, a powerful **court** order obtained **ex parte,** freezing the **defendant's** assets so that they cannot be shifted from the country; suing the defendant then becomes a worthwhile proposition. The term comes from the **leading case** Mareva Compania Naviera SA v International Bulk Carriers SA (1975). Serving a Mareva can have severe consequences for defendants, who may be individuals involved in some contractual or copyright dispute, as it restricts their access to their own bank accounts and often leaves them virtually penniless until the **case** is concluded. It may even be difficult for them to get legal help, as **solicitors** tend to require payment for their work from unfrozen funds. Marevas, like **Anton Pillers,** are regarded as nuclear weapons by solicitors; some consider their use oppressive and too widespread.

marriage

A civil or religious ceremony, registered by an authorized registrar, that creates the legal status of husband and wife. The minimum age for marriage is 16. There are four main types of marriage:

1 civil, where the ceremony usually takes place in a register office, in public and in front of witnesses;

2 Church of England, where it takes place in church and in front of **witnesses;**

3 Jewish and Quaker, where it is governed by the rules of those religions;

4 others, where the ceremony takes place in a registered building, in public and in front of witnesses.

See **age of consent.**

Master of the Rolls (MR)

A **judge** who is the President of the Civil Division of the **Court of Appeal.** The title gives the clue to his former humble station as keeper of records (rolls) of the **patents** and privileges granted by the Crown.

maternity rights

The rights of a woman against her employer which arise from her absence from work because of pregnancy. Depending on length of service and number of hours worked, she may be entitled to Statutory Maternity Pay and to return to her job after the birth; **trade unions** or citizens advice bureaux can advise on these points. Employers can recover maternity pay from the Maternity Pay Fund, financed by national insurance contributions. The wording of the relevant **law** is very complex. In 1983 the **Court of Appeal** agreed with an **Employment Appeal Tribunal** that the provisions were 'of inordinate complexity, exceeding the worst excesses of a taxing **statute**; we find that especially regrettable bearing in mind that they are regulating the everyday rights of ordinary employers and employees.'

matrimonial home

In England and Wales, the home where a husband and wife have lived together. If only one of the partners owns the home, the non-owner has certain rights of occupation which a **court** can enforce. One way to protect these rights is by registering a *Class F land charge* which warns prospective buyers that the non-owner has a right to live in the **property**.

See **battered wife; desertion; land charge**.

McKenzie Friend

In England and Wales, someone who sits next to a litigant-in-person in **court** and helps them by, for example, prompting, taking notes and quietly offering advice. The name derives from the **case** of McKenzie v McKenzie (1971), where the principle of such a helper was established, though it had existed since at least 1831. In 1991 the Appeal Court ruled that it was not for **judges** and **magistrates** to decide whether **litigants** needed the assistance of a McKenzie Friend; it was enough that the litigants considered they needed one.

McNaghten Rules

A set of principles which define how the **defence** of insanity may be proved in **court** in order to win a **verdict** of *not guilty by* *reason of insanity.* The rules say that accused people must prove that they suffered from a defect of reason arising from a serious mental disease and this meant they did not know what they were doing or that what they were doing was wrong. The rules were developed after the trial in 1843 of Daniel McNaghten, who killed the prime minister's secretary mistaking him for the prime minister. In this case insanity was proved. The rules act as a legal standard for insanity in Britain, Canada and many US states.

meliorations

In Scots law, improvements to **property** made by, for example, a **tenant**.

memorandum of association

A document which includes details of a company's name and **registered office,** purposes and initial share capital. It is lodged at the Companies Registry along with the **articles of association**.

mens rea

[Latin: guilty mind] In **criminal law,** the state of mind which the **prosecution** must prove the **accused** had when committing the **offence,** in order to get a conviction. To prove **murder** in English law, the prosecution must therefore not only show that the accused killed (the **actus reus**), but that he intended to kill or foresaw it as a likely result of his actions. The degree of likelihood can affect a **jury's verdict**—if they decide that the accused thought death was very unlikely, they might bring in a **manslaughter** verdict. To prove handling of stolen goods, the prosecution must prove not only that the goods were stolen, but that the accused knew they were stolen.

merchantable quality

A standard of quality which is implied in any sale of goods by a trader to a customer. If the goods do not meet this standard, the trader is breaking the **contract** which occurs when the sale is made. A rough test for merchantable quality is: *Should the goods have been sold in that condition, bearing in mind their price and description?* This means there is a lower standard for second-hand goods or those in a sale.

If a friend gives you a present which turns out to be of unmerchantable quality, he or she owns the rights in **law** to complain. He or she could, however, assign these rights to you by giving you a signed paper saying: 'By this document I assign to you all my rights arising out of the purchase from [company] on [date] of the enclosed gift.'

The term merchantable quality is antiquated and likely to be ousted by **satisfactory quality.**

See **fit for purpose.**

merits

If a **litigant** has a **defence** or claim *on the merits,* it means he or she can join battle on the substance of the matter, not merely on some point of **law.**

messuage

A house and its outbuildings, garden and orchard. An old-fashioned word still used in **leases** and **deeds.**

MI5

The Security Service, originally called Military Intelligence, which gathers information in Britain on people who may threaten national security.

MI6

The Secret Intelligence Service. It gathers intelligence abroad through agents attached to British embassies and high commisssions, using local informers who provide material on political, economic and military developments. Officially MI6 does not exist.

minority

The state of being a minor—a **child** under 18 (16 in Scotland), often referred to as an *infant.* Minors cannot validly make certain **contracts,** such as those for loans.

miscarriage of justice

A judicial cock-up.

See **sorry**.

misdescription

In a sale **contract,** a description of **property** which is false or inaccurate. If significant enough, it could be a breach of contract and lead to a claim for **damages** as well as making the contract unenforceable.

misdirection

A **judge's** incorrect direction to a **jury** on a point of **law;** it could lead to a conviction being quashed on **appeal.**

misrepresentation

During **contract** negotiations, a false **statement** by one **party** which induces the other to enter into the contract. This may lead to the contract being **voidable** and a claim for **damages**— even if the statement was made in good faith. A car dealer who told a customer that a vehicle had one previous owner would be making a misrepresentation if it turned out to be untrue.

See **voidable contract.**

missives

In Scotland, letters passing between a seller and a buyer (or their agents) as part of a private bargain for the sale and purchase of **land** or buildings. The seller offers the deal and the buyer accepts. The **contract** is then binding.

mistake

1 In a **criminal law case** where **mens rea** (intent) must be proved, a genuine mistake by the accused as to a matter of **fact.** This may provide a **defence,** for example to a charge of **theft,** if the **accused** genuinely believed that he or she was entitled to the **property.** On the other hand, someone who robbed Smith, genuinely thinking he was Jones, could not successfully claim mistake. Indeed, he could also be prosecuted for attempted robbery of Jones.

2 In **civil law,** a misunderstanding of **fact** which might, very rarely, invalidate a **contract** if the mistake concerned a matter which was fundamental to the contract.

mistrial

A trial which is **void** because of a fundamental error, such as a defect of **court** procedure.

month

In legal documents and **Acts of Parliament,** a calendar month not a lunar month.

moot

The trial of a hypothetical **case** among **law** students, hence a *moot point* meaning a debatable point. Often mispronounced *mute.*

mortgage

[Old French: dead pledge] A **contract** in which a lender (*mortgagee*) lends money to a borrower (*mortgagor*), the **security** for the loan being the borrower's **property.**

One theory on the derivation of the word is that the pledged **land** is dead to the borrower if the debt is not paid, and dead to the lender if it is.

MOT test

An annual test ordered by the Department of Transport on every motor vehicle which has been registered for three years or more. It covers brakes, tyres, steering, lights, seat belts, exhaust, indicators, washers, wipers, body and suspension. The test certificate does not certify roadworthiness; possession of a current MOT is no **defence** against **prosecution** for having an unroadworthy vehicle. A police officer can ask to see the MOT certificate whenever he or she could ask to see a **driving licence.** MOT is an abbreviation for **Ministry of Transport,** which no longer exists.

motion

A spoken request to a **judge** to make an order in a legal **case.**

moveable property (moveables)

In Scots law, **property** that is not **heritable,** such as animals, books, **copyright,** cash, machinery.

See **heritage.**

multiplepoinding

In Scots law, a legal **action** to determine the rights of the **parties** to **property** in dispute.

murder

[from Old English *morthor*: secret killing] Unlawful **homicide** which is not **manslaughter, infanticide** or causing death by **reckless driving.** For it to be murder, the victim must die within a year and a day of the **crime,** as a direct result of it. The **sentence** is **life imprisonment.** In Scotland and the USA, murder means homicide committed purposefully and knowingly.

See **mens rea.**

murmuring a judge

The **offence** in Scots law of saying nasty things about **judges. Prosecutions** are rare. The analogous term in English law is **scandalizing the judiciary.**

mutatis mutandis

[Latin: with the necessary changes] A shorthand way of saying that one document can easily be converted into another merely by altering a few words and phrases.

my learned friend

A term sometimes used in **court** by one **barrister** to refer to the opposition's barrister.

N

NACRO
The National Association for the Care and Resettlement of Offenders, a charity which works towards a more effective approach to preventing **crime** and more humane treatment of offenders. Its activities include the running of projects concerned with housing, employment training, youth training, and education and advice for offenders and people at risk.

nationality
The status of being a citizen of a particular country.

naturalization
The gaining of British citizenship by a certificate issued by the Home Secretary. The applicant must meet various criteria as to residence and swear an **oath** of allegiance to the Crown.

natural justice
A concept involving two main principles:

1 **judges** should be unbiased in hearing a case—they should have no financial or other **interest** in its outcome;

2 everyone has a right to be heard in their own cause—if you are directly affected by a decision you should be given the opportunity to state your **case** and know the other side's. Someone aggrieved by a breach of natural justice could seek **judicial review.**

negligence
1 In **criminal law,** failure to do something which the average responsible citizen would do, or doing something that such an individual would not do. This can be an element in some minor **crimes** such as careless driving, or more serious ones such as **manslaughter.**

2 In **civil law,** negligence means more than the idea of 'carelessness' in common speech. To succeed in an action for negligence, the **plaintiff** must prove that: (a) the defendant owed him or her a **duty of care**—for example, as between a driver and other road users, or a **solicitor** and a **client;** and (b) that the duty was breached in this **case;** and (c) that the breach caused damage to the plaintiff.

Professional advisers, such as solicitors or investment consultants, can often successfully defend a claim for negligence by saying that they merely offered advice and that it was for their client to accept or reject it or to take alternative advice. In such cases a plaintiff usually has to show some special relationship with the adviser in which he or she places great reliance on the adviser's opinions or actions. The more unworldly or stupid the client, the more he or she is likely to succeed in an **action** against a professional adviser.

Cases of medical negligence, where a patient is harmed by the act or omission of a doctor, may take many years to complete and can be something of a gamble unless the client is legally aided. During a House of Commons debate on whether no-fault compensation should be introduced, the MP Rosie Barnes cited the case of a woman whose husband was killed by hospital blunders. After a long fight she was awarded £250,000 with her costs, but the **defendant** appealed successfully. She lost the award and had to pay £130,000 costs.

See **contributory negligence; no-fault compensation.**

nem. con.

[Latin *nemine contradicente*: no one dissenting] The proposition is agreed unanimously.

next friend

An adult who is responsible for the conduct of a legal **action** started on behalf of a minor or mentally disordered individual.

See **minority.**

next of kin

Someone's close blood relations.

no case to answer

A submission in **court** on behalf of a **defendant** that the **plaintiff's** or prosecutor's case is so weak as not to be worth answering. If the **judge** agrees, in **civil cases** the defendant wins or in criminal cases is found **not guilty**.

no-fault compensation scheme

A scheme, not available in the UK, under which it is possible to claim **compensation** for injury without proving fault against a **defendant**. No-fault schemes operate on insurance principles.

Under UK **law** at present, to prove **negligence** for an injury is usually a long and expensive process unless one has **legal aid**. A professional being sued is usually insured up to the hilt and has large resources to fight the **case**. A no-fault scheme such as operates in New Zealand tends to produce less generous **awards** but in far more **cases**.

See **duty of care; nuisance; strict liability**.

noisy neighbours

See **nuisance**.

nolle prosequi

[Latin: to be unwilling to prosecute] In English law, the **Attorney-General's** decision to stop a **prosecution**. The term is often used for ironic effect in the comic novels of P G Wodehouse.

nonsuit

The **judge's** withdrawal of a **case** from a **jury**, recording a not-guilty **verdict**.

Notary Public

In Scotland, a **solicitor** authorized to administer **oaths**.

not guilty

An **accused's** denial of the charges, or a **verdict** that he or she did not commit the **offence** charged.

notice

1 Official publication of a decision of a government department, **court** etc.

2 Advance notification of intention to end an arrangement or **contract,** as in the phrase *you must give 2 weeks' notice.*

notice to quit

Formal notification from a **landlord** to a **tenant** (or vice versa) ending the tenancy on a certain date. It must be clear and unambiguous and, if the tenant lives in the **property,** must be in a form prescribed by **law** and set out the tenant's legal rights.

not proven

In Scottish **criminal law,** an intermediate **verdict** between **guilty** and **not guilty.** It has the same effect as not guilty but is appropriate where there is suspicion of guilt without conclusive **evidence.** The **accused** cannot be tried again for the same **offence.** It has been dubbed *Not guilty—but don't do it again.*

notwithstanding

Depending on the context, this means *despite; in spite of; yet; even though; however;* or *but.* The word is widely used by **lawyers** in documents, though few of their clients understand it readily. The term was coined in the Middle English period (1100–1500) from the Old English *withstand* (to oppose), and was not originally a lawyer's word. Its only essential use is as the answer to the crossword clue *shiny trousers.*

notwithstanding anything contained herein to the contrary

'Disregard what the rest of this document says, here is a really important bit which overrides the rest.' Careful **lawyers** avoid such blunderbuss phrases and set out any overriding exceptions under a heading saying *general exceptions.* Or they write *Despite paragraph 3 . . .*

no-win, no-fee

The practice widely used in the USA (where it is also called *contingency fee*) in which a client's **lawyer** does not get paid unless the **client** wins. This probably reduces the number of hopeless **cases** which come to **court**. It is not permitted in the UK since it could produce conflict of interest between a lawyer who wanted an early **out-of-court settlement** and a client who wanted to fight on.

now therefore

A **legalese** heading which means *here is some more writing for you to read.* The phrase is antiquated and redundant.

nuisance

1 In **civil law,** unreasonable interference with the use or enjoyment of neighbouring **property,** such as by noise, smell or smoke. The interference must be substantial for anyone to be able to make a **claim** for **damages** in **tort.** The **court** will look at what is **reasonable** in the circumstances. An all-night party next door once a fortnight might be reasonable, but three a week might not be. The usual **remedy** is an **injunction** to have the nuisance stopped. If a noise or vibration is persistent and seriously affects you, you can complain of *statutory nuisance* to the Environmental Health Department of your **local authority**. They may write to the individual concerned and say that they will be making independent checks with a view to **prosecution**. The maximum **fine** for domestic noise nuisance is £2 000, but offenders usually escape with a £50 fine.

In Scotland it is an **offence** not to stop making a noise when asked by the police, and offenders can face unlimited fines. In England and Wales police can only intervene if there is a **breach of the peace** or some other **crime** is suspected. The police cannot enter a property without a **warrant,** unless accompanied by a local authority Environmental Health Officer.

Under the Environmental Protection Act 1990, local authorities must 'take such steps as are reasonably practicable' to investigate complaints of statutory nuisance, including noise. A few local authorities run a 24-hour call-out service in response to this, but as local authorities get so many complaints, it is best to try to sort out the problem peacefully yourself with your neighbours. If you do make an official complaint, the local authority may ask you to keep a record of incidents and use it when asking **magistrates** to grant a Nuisance Order telling the neighbour to reduce the noise.

An alternative to using the local authority is to complain direct to the Clerk of the Magistrates' Court under Section 59 of the Control of Pollution Act 1974. Again it will be useful to show that you have asked the individual to reduce the noise and present a thorough record of all noise nuisance incidents.

A third course is to take a civil court **action** for noise nuisance under the **common law,** getting an **injunction** to stop the nuisance. This may prove expensive but is a powerful weapon in the hands of a group of citizens who are prepared to club together to foot the bill.

Someone whose health has been harmed by, for example, the activities of a polluter, may have a much better chance of winning an action for personal injury under nuisance than under negligence, since he or she would not have to prove that the polluter had breached any **duty of care.** The polluter's usual defence, that it had used the best practicable means of controlling the nuisance, would be useless in such a **case;** it could only be used if the local authority tried to prosecute for statutory nuisance.

See **abatement of nuisance.**

2 In **criminal law,** public nuisance includes obstruction of the **highway,** carrying on an offensive trade, and selling food unfit for people to eat.

null and void

Having no legal effectiveness. Since **null** and **void** mean exactly the same in this context, one of them on its own will always suffice. Using both is merely a waste of paper designed to impress non-lawyers.

nunc pro tunc

[Latin: now instead of then] In other words, the **judge** has backdated the decision.

O

oath

A formal declaration swearing the truth of a **statement** or **promise**. It is required for **affidavits** and before giving **court evidence**. The usual **witness's** oath has a ritual ring to it: 'I swear by Almighty God that the evidence which I shall give shall be the truth, the whole truth and nothing but the truth.' Those with religious objections to this formula may instead **affirm**—promise to tell the truth. The **law** recognizes various traditional or religious practices; a Chinese witness may break a plate, for example.

obiter dictum

[Latin: a remark in passing] A **judge's** opinion which is not essential to the **case** being tried. It does not create a **precedent** but can be quoted as persuasive in future cases. Often shortened to *obiter*.

obscene publications

Material whose effect tends to deprave or corrupt a significant proportion of those who are likely to read, see or hear it. It is an **offence** to publish an obscene article for money or to possess it for publication for money, whether or not anyone has been depraved or corrupted by it. The material need not be pornographic; it may depict or advocate violence, for example.

Material which is merely shocking or disgusting is not obscene, but it is for a **jury** in every case to decide whether something is obscene. Expert **witnesses** can be called. A common **defence** available in England and Wales is *public good,* where the **accused** tries to show that publication was in the interests of science, literature or the arts. The offence does not apply to radio and television.

As obscenity is difficult to prove, police in 1989 revived the old **common law** offence of *outraging public decency* and secured the conviction of a man who had exhibited ear-rings made from human fetal material. The **judge** directed that the jury must not hear from the array of expert witnesses who wished to tell them about art, saying that the jury should merely consider whether their own emotions had been outraged. They convicted on a 10–2 majority.

In the USA, the search for a definition of obscenity has not been without humour. Judge Woolsey contrasted 'dirt for dirt's sake' with the appropriateness he found in the language of James Joyce's 'Ulysses': 'The words which are criticised as dirty are old Saxon words known to almost all men and, I venture, to many women, and are such words as would be naturally and habitually used, I believe, by the types of folk whose life, physical and mental, Joyce is seeking to describe. In respect of the recurrent emergence of the theme of sex in the minds of his characters, it must always be remembered that his locale was Celtic and his season Spring.'

occupier

Someone in possession of **land** or buildings as owner or **tenant**. Trespassers can become lawful occupiers if the owner accepts **rent** from them.

offence

A **crime**. There are five main categories:

1 against **property**—eg **theft, deception,** criminal damage, **forgery, arson;**

2 against public order—eg riot, disorder, threatening behaviour, stirring up racial hatred;

3 against the individual—eg **homicide, rape, wounding, bodily harm; indecency, murder;**

4 against the state—eg **treason, sedition, official secrets** violations, terrorism;

5 concerning road traffic—eg careless driving, drunken driving, ignoring traffic signals.

offensive weapon

Anything made, adapted or meant to be used to cause someone physical injury. It is an **offence** to carry an offensive weapon in a public place without **reasonable** excuse. The need for **self defence** is not normally a good enough excuse unless danger is imminent. A folding penknife with a blade of 3 inches or less may be carried. Other knives are prohibited by the Criminal Justice Act 1988, though knives used for genuine religious or work reasons are permitted.

offer

See **contract**.

official receiver

Someone appointed by the Department of Trade and Industry to act in a **bankruptcy case** as interim receiver and manager of the **debtor's estate**.

Official Referee

A specialist **circuit judge** who deals with **cases** requiring detailed scrutiny of account books and other documentation.

official secrets

Information, documents or articles about state security or intelligence. It is an **offence** to disclose anything about the security services, even that the services themselves may be breaking the **law**. The Official Secrets Act 1989 ended the right to use *public interest* as a **defence** to an official secrets **charge** and stopped newspapers claiming prior publication of the material as a defence. The then Home Secretary described the measure as 'an essay in openness'.

Official Solicitor

A Supreme Court officer, such as a **solicitor,** who acts as **next friend** or **guardian ad litem** for someone who has no-one to help them.

Ombudsman

An independent official who considers allegations of injustice arising from maladministration by government departments, local government, banks, insurers etc. Individuals or corporate bodies may make complaints.

If an organization does something the wrong way, does something it should not have done, or fails to do something it should have done, that is maladministration. Maladministration includes neglect and unjustifiable delay, failure to follow the organization's own rules and procedures, failure to have proper procedures, malice, bias and unfair discrimination, failure to tell people their rights, failure to provide advice or information when reasonably requested, and providing inaccurate or misleading advice.

The local ombudsman deals with **local authorities,** while the parliamentary ombudsman (access to whom is via MPs only) deals with government departments. There are other ombudsmen for the National Health Service, banking and insurance.

The word ombudsman comes from the Scandinavian *Ombud,* a commissioner. The -man/-men suffix is entirely English.

See **Legal Services Ombudsman.**

open record

In Scots law, a document in which each of the **pursuer's** points of **fact** and **law** is followed by the **defender's answer.** In *record,* the stress is on the second syllable.

See **closed record.**

opinion

A statement, usually written, by a **solicitor** or **barrister** on a matter on which he or she has been consulted. When produced by a barrister it is called *counsel's opinion.*

oral examination

The questioning of someone, usually a **judgment debtor,** on **oath** in **court.** If the individual does not appear, he or she may be imprisoned. Oral examination has nothing to do with the debtor's teeth—unless he lies through them, of course.

See **judgment creditor.**

ouster injunction

A **court** order to exclude or dispossess someone from **property** to which they would otherwise have a legal right.

Outer House

In Scotland, part of the **Court of Session.** It is a **court of first instance,** ie it does not hear **appeals.**

out-of-court settlement

A settlement in a **civil case** in which the **parties** agree outside the courtroom. The agreement may cover **damages,** allocation of **costs,** and rules on whether settlement terms can be disclosed. The settlement is binding on the parties when they have agreed to it; the court then seals the order.

See **Tomlin order.**

outwith

Scots for *outside of, beyond* or *without.*

P

PACE

Acronym for *Police and Criminal Evidence Act 1984.*

See **detention.**

paralegal

Someone not qualified as a **solicitor** but who is experienced in certain kinds of legal work, such as housing, immigration, social security benefits. Some work in solicitors' offices, others in citizens advice bureaux. They can act as advocates before some **tribunals.** They may be **licensed conveyancers.**

paramour

In Scotland, an alleged adulterer named in **divorce** or judicial separation proceedings.

pardon

Withdrawal by the sovereign of a **sentence** or punishment, using the royal prerogative of mercy.

parental responsibility

The rights, powers, duties and responsibilities of a parent towards a child and its property under the Children Act 1989. More than one individual can have parental responsibility for the child. Married parents continue to share parental responsibility after a **divorce.** Unmarried mothers have parental responsibility, though the father will be able to share it by agreement or by **court** order. The parents of a child who goes into care share parental responsibility with the **local authority;** they lose it only if the child is adopted.

See **abortion; child; children in care.**

Parliament

The main law-making body of the UK—a combination of the sovereign, the **House of Commons** and the **House of Lords**.

See **community law**.

parol evidence

Spoken **evidence;** known as *parole evidence* in Scotland.

parole

Conditional release from prison of a prisoner who still has part of the **sentence** to serve. Prisoners can be considered for parole after serving a third of the sentence (or 6 months, if longer). A local review committee reports to the Parole Board which then advises the Home Secretary. In certain cases the Home Secretary may act on the advice of the local committee alone. Those on parole are supervised by a probation officer. The parole system in the UK was due to change radically as this book went to press: parole will be abolished for prisoners serving 4 years or less; they will be released automatically after half their sentence; and prisoners with longer sentences (except life sentences) will be considered for parole after serving half their sentences.

part

One of the people who make an agreement, as in: *This agreement is between John Grumble of the first part and Harold Chisel of the second part.*

particulars

Details of an allegation or **claim. Solicitors** may ask for *further and better particulars* if a **pleading** is ambiguous or vague.

parts and pertinents

In Scots law, everything (except certain Crown rights) connected with or forming part of **lands** which are conveyed.

party

[Old French *partie*: a faction] A **litigant** or one of the sides named in a **deed** or **contract**.

See **third party**.

partnership

An association of two or more people formed to carry on business together, with or without a partnership agreement drawn up by a **solicitor**. In most partnerships the partners lack limited liability so they are individually responsible for all the firm's debts. This, and the scope for mistrust and **fraud,** makes partnership an unattractive option; it has been described as 'the worst bloody ship that ever sailed.'

A *partnership at will* is one that can be ended by one of the **parties** giving **reasonable notice** to the others.

See **limited liability company**.

passing off

Selling one's goods or services so that they appear to be those of another business. This can lead to a **claim** for **damages** even if the passing off is unwitting. Passing off may take the form of mimicking design or packaging. Lord Diplock put forward a fivefold test for a passing-off action to succeed. There must be: '(1) a **misrepresentation,** (2) made by a trader in the course of trade, (3) to prospective customers of his or ultimate consumers of goods or services supplied by him, (4) which is calculated to injure the business or **goodwill** of another trader (in the sense that this is a reasonably foreseeable consequence) and (5) which causes actual damage to a business or goodwill of the trader by whom the **action** is brought or . . . will probably do so.'

patent

A right of monopoly, granted by the Crown through the Patent Office, to exploit an invention. The patent application must prove that the invention is new, not obvious, and is capable of industrial use. A patent remains valid for 20 years from the date of application if regular fees are paid, though a UK patent is only valid in the UK. Infringement of the patent can lead to a **claim** for **damages**. A patent is a form of **intellectual property**.

Patents County Court

A **court** in Wood Green, north London, which aims to deliver cheaper, quicker and more informal **justice** than the **High Court** for individuals and small businesses who claim their **patents** have been infringed.

payment into court (payment-in)

In an English **civil case,** a **defendant's** offer of money in an attempt to satisfy the **plaintiff's** claim. It is paid into a special **court** account. The plaintiff has 21 days to accept or reject the offer. If accepted, the plaintiff also gets his or her **costs** and the **case** ends. If rejected, the trial **judge** (and **jury,** if any), does not normally hear of the offer and the case goes forward. If the final **award** is the same as or less than the payment-in, the plaintiff will usually have to pay the defendant's costs from the date of the payment-in as well as his or her own costs. (In the case of a legally aided plaintiff, the costs will come from his or her winnings.)

Payment-in forces a plaintiff to balance the amount offered against a winner-takes-all gamble. This adds to the stress borne by an individual **litigant,** whereas it may be all in a day's work for a big opponent like an insurance company. In addition, the **solicitors** of legally aided clients may virtually force them to settle by saying that the Legal Aid Board would regard the payment-in as **reasonable** and would refuse to fund any further **action**.

The Scottish equivalent is a Minute of Tender.

pecuniary legacy

A gift of money by **will**.

Pelican crossing

A pedestrian crossing controlled by lights. The signals have the same meaning as traffic lights except that a flashing amber signal follows the red stop signal. When the amber light flashes, drivers must give way to any pedestrians on the crossing. Parking or overtaking is not allowed in the area marked by the zigzag lines on the approach to the crossing.

penalty
Punishment for an **offence.**

peppercorn rent
A **rent** of a peppercorn, that is, a nominal rent. Such a tiny amount satisfies the rule that in some kinds of **contract** there must be *consideration*—'I let this property to you for £5 a week.'

performance of contract
The fulfilling of duties under a **contract.** A **court** may order *specific performance,* ie that a **party** to the **contract** must fulfil his or her duties under it, or an injunction restraining non-performance which effectively secures performance.

per incuriam
[Latin: through lack of care] A polite way of describing a **court** decision which mistakenly ignored a binding **precedent** or a relevant **law.**

periodical allowance
In Scotland, periodic payments made by one **marriage** partner to another under a **court** order after **divorce.**

perjury
The **offence** of deliberately giving false **evidence** during judicial proceedings in **court** or in an **affidavit.** The offence can be committed by anyone who has taken the **oath** or affirmed.

person
An individual (known as a *natural person*) or a **corporation** (known as a *juristic or artificial person*). Hence the use of *persons* in **Acts of Parliament** where *people* would be more everyday English.

personal bar
See **estoppel**.

personal property (personalty)
Any **property** which is not **land** or the rights associated with land. **Leases** are personal property, as are moveable goods, known as *chattels*. A gift of personal property by **will** is a **legacy**.

See **intellectual property; real property**.

personal representative
Someone appointed to deal with a **deceased's estate** in accordance with a **will** or the rules of **intestacy**.

personal service
See **service**.

per stirpes
[Latin: by the roots] The term used for a way of distributing a share of **property**—usually by **will**—so that if the individual due to receive it under the will dies before doing so, the share is split equally between their children.

perverse verdict
A **jury verdict** that ignores the weight of evidence or defies a **judge's** direction.

The term was used in 1991 when two men who had helped release a spy from prison were acquitted despite admitting they had done it—apparently the jury decided that the **case** should not have been brought and that the men's action was justified by wider considerations than mere **law**.

perverting the course of justice
Doing anything that impedes or defeats the aims of **justice**. This **offence** includes destroying **evidence**, making false **statements** to the police, or influencing or threatening jurors.

It is not an offence to offer **compensation** to a victim of **crime** in return for agreement not to take proceedings, but if the victim has already made a statement to police, it is an offence to induce the victim to withdraw or change it. No offence is committed in offering money to someone not to **sue** in the **civil courts.**

Conspiracy to pervert the course of justice occurs when people get together to produce false evidence, rig a trial etc.

petition

A written application to the **court** for a legal **remedy,** such as **damages** or an **injunction**. One who puts forward such a petition is a *petitioner*. Hence *divorce petition, bankruptcy petition.*

picketing

During a **trade dispute,** attendance by employees at or near their own place of work in order to exchange information or dissuade others from working or delivering supplies. Pickets at their own place of work cannot be sued for inducing other employees to break their **contracts**. *Secondary picketing—* picketing away from their place of work—is outlawed. A Department of Employment Code of Practice on picketing gives detailed guidance and has legal status. It says: 'pickets and their organizers should ensure that in general the number of pickets does not exceed six at any one entrance to a workplace.' In practice, the police have considerable discretion in deciding how many pickets are appropriate.

It is an **offence** for a picket to intimidate someone who wants to work by, for example, persistently following him, watching his house, or hiding his tools and clothes.

place of safety order

In Scots law, an order from the local **justice of the peace** or **sheriff** which allows social workers to remove a **child** from its parents if emergency measures are necessary for its protection. This is normally followed within 7 days by a **hearing** by officials of the children's panel which parents may attend. The analogous order in England is an **emergency protection order.**

See **children in care.**

plaint

[From complaint] A written **statement** used to start a **county court action.** It sets out the cause of action. The action will be given a number—the *plaint number.* The next step is for the court to issue a **summons.**

plaintiff

[From Latin *plangere*: to lament] A **person** applying for a **remedy**—such as **damages**—against someone in a **civil action.**

plea

A **statement** in **court** by or on behalf of an **accused** in response to the **charge,** eg **guilty** or **not guilty.**

plea bargain

An agreement between **prosecution** and **defence** that if, for example, the **accused** pleads **guilty** to one **charge** a more serious charge will be dropped. Sometimes **judges** take part in this process informally in their rooms, saying that they will pass a lighter **sentence** if the accused pleads guilty and gets it over with. The accused is not present during negotiations and is not obliged to agree.

pleading

In a civil **action,** a written **statement** served by one **party** on the other. It includes the allegations and states the **relief** required, such as **damages.** The aim is to give the other side notice of the issues to be proved at the trial, so that **surprise** cannot take place.

plea in mitigation

A **plea** by the **defence,** after conviction but just before **sentence,** which seeks to reduce the severity of the sentence. Family circumstances, **hearsay,** and character witnesses can all be used at this time.

plea-in-law

In Scots law, statements of the legal principles which underpin the **pursuer's case.**

poinding

/pɪndɪŋ/

In Scots law, the seizing of a **debtor's** goods so that they can be sold to benefit the **creditor**. It could follow the creditor's successful **action** in **court**. The goods seized must be sold at auction in a **warrant sale**.

poinding of the ground

In Scots law, a form of **diligence** which a **creditor** who holds a **security** over a **debtor's land** can use to seize **moveable property** on the land, but not the land itself.

poison pen letters

See **sending distressing letters**.

Police Complaints Authority (PCA)

A body, headed by a **judge,** which supervises police investigations into complaints against police officers, and considers whether disciplinary action is necessary. In the three years to 1990 the PCA completed 7273 **cases** involving a total of 16712 complaints. Of these, 758 led to criminal or disciplinary proceedings, and 33 led to one or more officers being prosecuted. In serious cases, the disciplinary **tribunals** are held in public.

police committee

A body made up of county councillors and **magistrates** which is responsible for maintaining adequate and efficient police forces in a police area such as a county or group of counties. In counties the police committee is the police authority. The police committee has the major say in appointing the Chief Constable but does not direct police operations or exercise managerial control.

police officer

Someone who has agreed to serve the Crown as an officer of the peace. Technically a police officer is independent— neither a Crown servant nor **local authority** employee. Under the Police Act 1964, a police officer must not be a member of a **trade union** nor of any association which seeks to control or influence police pay, pensions or conditions of service.

political asylum

Refuge granted by a state to someone who would be liable to persecution because of religion, nationality, political opinions or race if he or she returned to the country of origin.

pollution

See **nuisance**.

polygamy

The practice of having more than one **marriage** partner. A polygamous marriage contracted in England and Wales cannot be valid under English **law**. If contracted abroad, it will only be valid under English law if both partners were domiciled outside England and Wales at the time.

See **domicile**.

post mortem

[Latin: after death] The examination of a body in order to establish the cause of death. Also known as *autopsy*.

See **inquest**.

power of attorney

An authority given by one individual to another (known as the **attorney**) to act on his or her behalf to receive debts, pay bills etc, but not to do things which require the personal presence of that individual, such as to sign a **will** or appear in **court**. Power of attorney must be given by **deed**. It comes to an end if the giver becomes mentally incapable. The usual cost is £25–100. If major matters are involved, such as selling a house, or if mental incapacity seems likely—say if the giver's memory is fading badly—it is best to create an *enduring power of attorney* which acts after the giver has become mentally unfit to handle his or her own affairs. The enduring power can be added to an ordinary power of attorney. In Scotland this is now automatic unless the giver has specifically stated in the original document that it shouldn't happen.

power of sale

The right of a lender (*mortgagee*) to sell a mortgaged **property** if the borrower (*mortgagor*) has broken the agreement by, for example, falling more than two months behind with interest payments. If the property is sold, the lender must normally act with **reasonable** care to obtain a good price and must repay any surplus money (after clawing back the loan) to the borrower.

See **mortgage**.

power of search

The right to search people or **property**. In most circumstances, the police (or other officials such as **Inland Revenue** investigators) may only search premises if they suspect there has been a **serious arrestable offence** and they have a **search warrant** from a magistrate. They do not need a search warrant to enter and search a place where someone who has committed an arrestable offence may be hiding, nor in pursuit of terrorism or drug **offences**. The police can stop and search any individual or vehicle found in a public place for stolen or prohibited articles.

Practice Directions

Statements made by the head of a **court**, such as the head of the Family Division, which tell the courts within his or her **jurisdiction** what procedure to follow. To get an abuse of court procedure stopped, pressure groups may find it easier to lobby for a Practice Direction than to get an **Act of Parliament** changed.

precedent

The principles underlying a **judgment** or decision in a higher **court** which lower courts and, generally, courts at the same level, are bound to follow. They are usually recorded in **law reports**. The decisions of **county** and **magistrates' courts** do not create precedents. The House of Lords and the Criminal Divisions of the Court of Appeal are not bound to follow precedents they have set.

Lord Denning, who retired as Master of the Rolls in 1982, argued that **judges** should ignore precedent when they considered it created injustice, but many of his precedent-bucking decisions in the **Court of Appeal** were overturned by his more conservative brethren in the **House of Lords**.

In a **case** reported in 1344, Judge Sharshulle mentioned a previous similar case but said 'No precedent is of such force as justice or that which is right.' This does not seem to have created much of a precedent, but judges who consider that a precedent will cause injustice may try to find a way of distinguishing the **case** before them from the case in which the precedent was laid down; then they can impose a different judgment.

A precedent is said to be *in point* if it settled the same question of **law** which now lies before the court, or *persuasive* (ie, not binding) if it was decided by a court of equal or lower rank.

See **common law; stare decisis**.

precognition
In Scots law, a **statement** by a **witness** of the evidence which he or she can give.

prejudice
Legal jargon for *alter* or *affect,* as in: *This does not prejudice your legal rights.*

See **without prejudice**.

pre-marital contract
A legally binding **contract** before **marriage,** spelling out the main responsibilities and rights of the partners. It would include details of what the partners would get in the event of a **divorce,** thus avoiding a court-imposed solution that might be against their wishes.

At present, these contracts are probably not enforceable but might be taken into account by a **court**. The **Law Society** has recommended they become enforceable in England and Wales provided both parties took legal advice before making the contract. Reviews would have to occur regularly or when events like the birth of a **child** took place.

See **cohabitation contracts**.

presents

In a **deed, legalese** for *present statements,* as in: *By these presents I give you my antique wardrobe* or *Know all men by these presents.*

presumption of innocence

The assumption under English law that anyone charged with a **crime** is innocent until proved **guilty.**

previous convictions

Offences committed before. There are several circumstances in which a **judge** may allow the **prosecution** in a criminal **case** to reveal an **accused's** previous convictions:

1 If the accused has tried to show that he or she is of good character or has attacked the character of **witnesses,** for example by accusing the police of fabricating **evidence.**

2 If the accused has given evidence against someone else charged in the same case.

3 If the previous offences were strikingly similar to the ones charged and are relevant to the current case.

Previous convictions of **witnesses** can be cited to discredit them. In **civil cases,** previous convictions of the **parties** can be cited if they are relevant.

prima facie case

[from Latin *prima facies*: first appearance] A **litigant** has a prima facie case if the **evidence** in his or her favour is strong enough for an opponent to be called to answer it.

principal

1 In **civil law,** someone who acts on behalf of someone else.

2 In **criminal law,** the individual who commits a **crime** (*principal in first degree*) or who aids and abets a criminal (*principal in the second degree*).

privacy

The right not to have one's peace invaded by others—this right does not exist in English **law**. Laws on trespass, **harassment** of **tenants, confidence** and **defamation** give indirect protection of privacy.

A recent **case** illustrates the problems. Gorden Kaye, the actor, was badly injured in a storm. Recovering from brain surgery in a hospital's private ward, he was confronted by a newspaper photographer who took pictures without his consent. Kaye tried for an **injunction** to stop publication, but failed on **appeal,** though one of the **judges** described the paper's action as 'a monstrous invasion of privacy'. All Kaye achieved was an injunction preventing the paper from implying that he had given his consent. If, however, he had gone to **court** alleging trespass, he would have had a much better chance. He could have claimed infringement of his lawful possession of the private ward and could then have stopped the paper printing the photographs, using the legal maxim that no-one may profit from wrongs they have committed.

See **trespassers will be prosecuted.**

private law

See **civil law.**

private prosecution

A **prosecution** by a private individual for a criminal act. These sometimes occur when the **Crown Prosecution Service** has declined to prosecute, perhaps for lack of **evidence.** The **Director of Public Prosecutions** can take over a private prosecution and go forward with it or abandon it.

privilege

1 Parliamentary privilege: the right of members of the **House of Commons** and **House of Lords** to completely free speech during parliamentary proceedings, giving them protection from civil claims for **damages** (arising out of, for example, **libel**) and criminal prosecution (for example, for revealing **official secrets**). The privilege does not apply if members make the same remarks outside **Parliament.** Privileged statements

may be freely repeated by people not protected by the primary right of privilege, though it is wise to stick closely to the original words.

2 The right of a **witness** (though not an **accused**) to refuse to answer certain kinds of questions. There is a *privilege against self-incrimination*—the witness cannot be asked questions if the answer might incriminate him or her. And there is *legal professional privilege* under which a **lawyer** can refuse to disclose communications with a **client** and vice versa. Journalists, however, have rarely succeeded in convincing the **courts** that they can refuse to answer questions in court about their sources; they can be imprisoned for contempt. Communications between people in a confidential relationship, such as a husband and wife, are privileged—a court cannot force a wife to testify against her husband, or vice versa.

See **contempt of court**.

privity of contract

A rule saying that only the **parties** to a **contract** can **sue** and be sued over it. A contract cannot give rights to, nor impose liabilities on, others.

probate

The official validating of a **will**. The **executor** of the will applies to the Family Division of the **High Court** for a certificate confirming that the will is valid and that the executor has the right to administer the **estate** of the **deceased**. A probate **action** is a court **case** which determines whether a disputed will is valid or gets a probate certificate revoked. In Scotland the term for probate is *confirmation*.

probation order

A method of dealing with offenders where, instead of a prison **sentence,** a **court** may order the offender to be supervised for a fixed period by a probation officer. Offenders have a choice as to whether to accept probation.

pro bono work

[From Latin *pro bono publico*: for the public good] Work which some **lawyers** do without pay on behalf of penniless **litigants**. Some of the work is co-ordinated by the Free Representation Unit, a charity which attracts **barristers** and a few **solicitors** to give their time. **Clients** are referred to it by citizens advice bureaux etc. Only a tiny proportion of lawyers undertake pro bono work.

process

A **court** document which includes copies of all the documents in a court **case** from, for example, the **summons** up to the final judgment.

procurator fiscal (the fiscal)

In Scotland, the public prosecutor in the **sheriff court** and in the district court—a full-time civil servant. The fiscal must be a **solicitor** or **advocate**. The police report the details of a **crime** to the fiscal who decides whether to prosecute, subject to the control of the Crown Office, a kind of Scottish **Crown Prosecution Service**. He or she can examine **witnesses** and ask police to search for harder **evidence**. In this respect the fiscal's role is akin to a French examining magistrate's. The fiscal also deals with **fatal accident inquiries;** there are no **coroners** in Scotland.

procuring breach of contract

Deliberately persuading X to break a **contract** which X has made with Y, who could then mount a civil **action** for **damages** against the **person** doing the persuading.

product liability

The liability which manufacturers and others have towards private customers to whom they supply their products. A manufacturer who supplied a defective product which killed, injured or caused damage could be sued under the Consumer Protection Act 1987.

prohibited degrees of relationship

Family relationships in which the **law** prohibits **marriage**. For example, a woman may not marry her grandfather, uncle or nephew. A man may not marry his grandmother, aunt or niece.

promise

A voluntary undertaking given by one **person** to another to do or not do something. It is not legally binding unless set out as a **contract** or **deed**.

proof

1 The means of establishing the truth of a **fact** to the satisfaction of a **court**. Proof includes documentary **evidence** and **statements** from credible **witnesses**.

2 In **solicitors'** slang, a witness's statement. *Putting someone to proof* means testing their evidence in person, for example in **cross-examination**.

3 In Scots law, a court hearing on a question of fact by a **Lord Ordinary** sitting alone in a **civil case**.

See **burden of proof**.

proof before answer

In Scots law, a procedure in which the **court** hears full **evidence** on a point of **law** before making a decision on the point at issue.

property

Something owned or possessed.

See **intellectual property; personal property; real property**.

prosecution

1 The term used to describe someone who acts as prosecutor. Hence: *The prosecution said . . .*

2 The taking of any **suit** or **action** at **law,** though nowadays the term is generally confined to the taking of criminal proceedings against an **accused**.

See **private prosecution**.

prostitution

The offering by a woman to a man of **sexual intercourse** or other sexual activities with her in return for money. This is not an **offence,** though associated activities such as **soliciting** are.

proving a will

See **probate**.

provision

A demand, **condition** or stipulation in a legal document.

proviso

A clause in a legal document which qualifies or makes conditional some other **provision**.

See *applying the proviso*.

provocation

Words or conduct which suddenly cause someone to lose self-control and act in an unpremeditated way. Provocation is sometimes offered as a **defence** to a **charge** of **murder,** when the **jury** may, if convinced, bring in a **verdict** of **manslaughter**. A jury must be convinced that a **reasonable** individual of the same kind as the **accused** would have been likely to do the same as the accused. The defence of provocation is said to be more easily available to men since they tend to react with an instant loss of self-control when, for example, killing their wives. Women who have been battered or abused over a long period of time may be unable to react suddenly for fear of retaliation. If they kill later, **courts** have regarded this as premeditated murder.

proximate cause

An imprecise term which may mean almost anything from the direct cause of an event to an indirect cause. The concept can be important in a **claim** for **negligence,** where the **plaintiff** may need to prove that the **defendant's** actions 'caused' the event complained of, while the defendant may claim there is some break in the chain of **causation** which led to the event.

public examination

During **bankruptcy** proceedings, a **court** inquiry into a **debtor's** conduct, dealings and **property**. The debtor must attend and answer questions on **oath**.

public policy

The interests of society. **Contracts** that contravene public policy are **void**—eg a contract to commit a **crime**. A contract which places undue restrictions on someone's right to earn a living may also be against public policy and unenforceable.

See **void contract**.

Public Trustee

A public official who administers small **estates** which do not have any other **executor**.

puff

Sales talk which no-one should take seriously. If a garage advertised a vehicle as 'the best car in Manchester', everyone would know they didn't believe it—it would be a mere puff, made for the sake of effect. A purchaser could not claim a breach of **contract** if the car proved not to be the best. But if the garage said the car's mileage was 30 000 and this turned out to be false, the purchaser could **sue** for **misrepresentation**.

puisne judge

/'pjuːnɪ/

[From Old French *puisne*: younger] An ordinary **judge** of the **High Court**.

punctuation

See **sentence length**.

pupil

In Scotland, at **common law**, a girl up to 12 years old or a boy up to 14. Such **children** are said to be *in pupillarity*.

purport

To claim or pretend to be true or official.

pursuer

In Scotland, the **person** suing in a **civil case**. The equivalent of **plaintiff** in English law.

putative

Believed, reputed or supposed.

Q

quantum
Lawyers' shorthand for an amount, usually of **damages**, eg: *I don't know what the quantum would be.*

quash
To nullify, as in: *The judge quashed the conviction.* The effect is to unconvict the convicted.

quasi-contract
An act or event from which, despite the lack of a **contract**, a contractual obligation arises. For example, if A has been paying a sum to B under the mistaken belief that it was due, B must repay.

Queen's Bench Division
See **High Court**.

Queen's Counsel
See **barrister**.

Queen's evidence
Evidence for the **prosecution** given by someone who confesses guilt but then turns **witness** against his or her **accomplices** in the hope of a reduced **sentence**. **Courts** consider it less reliable since the **witness** will try to enlarge his accomplices' guilt to reduce his own. If the evidence is uncorroborated the **judge** should alert the **jury** to the danger of convicting on it alone.

See **corroboration**.

quiet enjoyment

A **landlord's** duty to allow a **tenant** to use the **land** without disturbance or interference from the landlord. Though the phrase is often found in **leases,** it is unnecessary, as the right to quiet enjoyment is implied in every lease unless specifically excluded.

R

R

Abbreviation in **law reports** and elsewhere for *Rex* or *Regina* (Latin for *King* and *Queen* respectively). A criminal **prosecution** by the state, represented by the monarch, against Smith would be listed as *R v Smith.*

racial discrimination

Discrimination because of colour, race, nationality or ethnic origin. Several **offences** are possible under the various Race Relations Acts:

1 incitement to racial hatred, which may include using threatening behaviour or words, publishing threatening material, presenting a play which uses threatening words, and providing a radio or television programme involving threatening images or sounds;

2 discrimination in public places and in respect of services, facilities, goods, employment, accommodation and advertisements;

3 discrimination in clubs with more than 25 members.

Many **defences** to the **charges** are possible and **prosecutions** are unusual. At present it is not an offence to discriminate against someone because of their religion. A prosecution failed in 1991 against a man who asked a job centre to send him only non-Muslim applicants.

rape

Sexual intercourse by a man with a woman without her consent, or if consent was obtained through force, fear or **fraud,** or through her mental inability to understand her consent. If there is **reasonable** doubt as to whether the man honestly believed the woman consented, he will be acquitted. A man can be convicted of raping his wife.

According to research evidence, most rapes are committed by husbands against their wives, with rape by boyfriends or acquaintances being the next most common.

In offences connected with rape or attempted rape, the victim's identity cannot normally be reported, nor can the **defendant's** until conviction. In the UK, questioning in **court** about the woman's sexual history is restricted by **law**. This differs from practice in some states of the USA where every detail of a woman's sexual history is fair game for the defence.

There is no offence of rape by a man upon another man, nor by a woman upon a man—the law regards this as **indecent assault,** punishable by a maximum of 10 years in prison. Rape of a woman is punishable by **life imprisonment.**

See **common law.**

ratio decidendi
[Latin: the reason for deciding] The legal principles by which a **court** decides a **case**. Often shortened to *ratio.*

re
See **in re.**

real property (real estate or realty)
Land, buildings and intangible assets like **easements**.

reasonable
One of the most important words in the language of the **law,** but deliberately left undefined in the many **Acts of Parliament** which use it. What is reasonable in any case depends on the circumstances and on **precedent. Courts** often apply a *reasonable man test,* also known as the *man-on-the-Clapham-omnibus test:* 'What would a reasonable man have done in these circumstances?' 'Was the standard of care provided reasonable given the skill of the surgeon?' The word is similar in its imprecision to *substantial* and *satisfactory,* also widely used in the language of the law.

Reasonable has been imprecise since Magna Carta in 1215 which spoke of the king's power to levy reasonable aid. The sum soon had to be defined because of King John's greed. In 1952 **Lord Chief Justice** Goddard commented: 'I have never yet heard any court give a real definition of what is reasonable doubt, and it would be better if that expression was not used.'

reasonable force

The amount of force it is **reasonable** to use in order to defend yourself or your **property** against attack or trespass, or to lawfully **arrest** a criminal or suspect. It is lawful to use force not merely to counter an attack but to ward off an attack you honestly believe is imminent. In defending yourself (or your property or an individual) you may only do what is necessary for the defence. So it would not be wise to shoot a retreating intruder in the back. It helps if you can show that what you did was spontaneous (in the heat of the moment) and it may help to show that you tried to retreat or call off the fight. If you carry a stick 'just in case' and use it in **self defence** you may come off worse in any **prosecution** for **assault** than if you pick up a stick lying on the ground and hit the attacker in self defence.

reckless

A word with a muddy meaning in the **law.** In a **rape** trial, recklessness might mean that the man was indifferent to whether the woman consented, therefore he had the **mens rea** to commit rape. In other **offences** it might mean being aware of the risk that a particular consequence would stem from one's behaviour but pressing on with it regardless.

See **causing death by reckless driving.**

reclaiming motion

In Scots law, an **appeal** to the **Inner House.** If the appeal is on a question of **fact,** the **judges** do not re-hear the **evidence** but read a transcript of it. If the appeal is on a question of **law,** the judges will only be concerned with legal arguments not the facts of the **case.** Their decision either *adheres* to the original **interlocutor** (refuses the appeal) or *recalls* it (allows the appeal and substitutes a new **judgment**).

recognizance

An offender's agreement to pay a sum of money to the **court** if he or she breaks certain conditions: *He was bound over to keep the peace on his own recognizance of £50.*

recorder

A **barrister** or **solicitor** acting as a part-time **judge** and sitting mainly in the **Crown Court**.

reduction

In Scots law, the setting aside of a **decree**.

redundancy

An employee's loss of a job because the employer no longer needs his or her services. In **law** several conditions have to be met before you can claim a statutory redundancy pay-off including:

1 the employers must be stopping or intending to stop the business in which you are employed; or

2 they must be transferring the business in which you work to another location; or

3 they must need fewer workers to do the work in the place where you are employed; and

4 you must have been continuously employed in the business for 104 weeks excluding any time you were under 18 or over 65 (60 if female).

There are other rules covering lay-offs and short-time working.

The pay-off is based on length of service, though many employers offer more generous terms.

re-enter the premises

A phrase used in tenancy agreements to set out a **landlord's** right to repossess a **property** if, for example, the **rent** is not paid after a certain time.

registered design

A design registered at the Patent Office in order to obtain monopoly rights over the outward appearance of a thing (though not the idea behind it). The protection can last 15 years.

registered land

Land whose **title** is registered at the **Land Registry.**

registered office

A company's official address as registered with the Companies Registry. The address must appear on company letter-heads.

register of members

A roll of names, addresses and shareholdings of members of a registered company. It must be readily available for inspection, usually at the company's **registered office,** for at least 2 hours daily, and may not remain closed on more than 30 working days a year.

registration as citizen

See **citizenship.**

registering a birth

The compulsory giving of information about a birth to a Registrar of Births and Deaths, within 42 days of the birth (21 days in Scotland). The information must consist of the name and sex of the **child,** its parentage, and the date and place of birth. Responsibility for registration lies with a parent of the child, or an individual present at the birth, or the occupier of the premises where the birth occurred, or someone who has charge of the child.

registering a death

The compulsory giving of information about a death to a Registrar of Births and Deaths, within 5 days of the death (14 days if written notice is given). The information must consist of the name, sex, address and occupation of the **deceased,** the cause of death, and the date and place of death. Responsibility for registration lies with any relative of the deceased, anyone present at the death, or the occupier of the premises where death occurred.

regulated tenancy

A form of residential letting by a non-resident private **landlord**. Most residential lettings which began before 15 January 1989 are regulated tenancies, whether they are furnished or not. In a regulated tenancy:

1 the landlord cannot evict without a **court** order for possession;

2 if the **tenant** dies, the **marriage** partner (or another family member who has been living there for at least 2 years) will normally have a right to take over the tenancy;

3 the landlord or tenant can apply to a rent assessment committee to have a fair rent registered—this is the most that can be charged until the amount is reviewed or cancelled;

4 the landlord is responsible for major repairs.

A court can give the landlord a possession order on 10 mandatory grounds and 9 discretionary grounds under the Rent Act 1977. The mandatory grounds, where the court must give the landlord possession, include:

1 the landlord let the home with the intention of returning to live there again;

2 the landlord wishes to retire to the **property;**

3 the landlord was a member of the armed forces when the letting was made and intends to live in the house in the future.

The discretionary grounds, where the court will only grant a possession order if it thinks it is reasonable, include:

1 the tenant has not paid rent or has broken some other term of the tenancy;

2 the tenant has caused **nuisance** or annoyance to neighbours;

3 the tenant has assigned or sub-let the property without consent;

4 the tenant has damaged the property or furniture.

rehearing

A second hearing of a **case**. It may occur, for example, in the **Crown Court** if the **accused appeals** against conviction by the **magistrates' court**. The **evidence** is heard again and new evidence may be cited. This differs from a rehearing in the **Court of Appeal** where the **court** will re-read the evidence but will not normally allow fresh evidence.

relief

A legal method of enforcing, protecting or recovering rights, or of getting **compensation** for their breach. Relief may include **damages** and **injunction**.

remainder

A legal **interest** in **land** that only comes into its own when a prior interest ends. For example, a **will** might leave a house in **trust** to A during his lifetime but when he dies the trust gives it to B. B's interest in the house is called a *remainder* and he is called a *remainderman*.

remand

To release an **accused** on bail or commit him or her to **custody** during an adjournment. Custody may be a prison, remand centre or police station. Juvenile suspects may be remanded on bail or in a **local authority** secure unit or an adult prison. Remands of juveniles to prison will be phased out by 1995 as a result of a spate of suicides in prison.

remedy

See **relief**.

remission

A cut in a prison **sentence** because of, for example, good behaviour.

See **parole**.

remuneration certificate

A certificate from the **Law Society** stating what is a proper amount for a **solicitor** to charge. Getting a remuneration certificate is a way of having your solicitor's bill checked if you think it is too high, but you can only get one if court proceedings were not issued. At your request your solicitor must apply for a certificate provided:

1 you have not paid the bill or your solicitor has taken off his costs from money held on your behalf; and

2 not more than a month has passed since your solicitor said you could ask for a certificate.

When it receives the solicitor's file on the matter, the Law Society writes to you for your comments.

If your solicitor gave you an estimate, that will normally be the most the Law Society will allow to be charged.

If you have to pay an opponent's costs, you can have them checked through **taxation** or by asking your opponent to get a remuneration certificate.

rent

A **tenant's** payment to a **landlord** under the terms of a **lease** or tenancy agreement. Payments are recorded in a rent book or rent card which a landlord must normally provide.

repeal

The revoking of a **law,** or part of it, by **Parliament** passing another law.

repel

In Scots law, to reject a **plea-in-law.**

See **interlocutor; sustain.**

representation

1 A statement made by, for example, a member of the public objecting to or commenting upon a proposal of a planning or other authority.

2 In **contract law,** a statement. Someone persuaded to enter a contract by a false statement may be able to win **damages** or have the contract set aside for **misrepresentation.**

representative action

See **class action.**

repugnancy

Inconsistency in a document. **Courts** interpret inconsistency in line with the **parties'** main intention—if they can work it out.

rescission

The cancellation of a **contract** to restore the **parties** to their pre-contract position.

rescue

Action to save people or **property** in danger. People are not legally obliged to rescue others, though the master of a ship has a legal duty to help people in danger at sea. Someone injured trying to rescue people could claim **damages** for **negligence** from the **person** who caused the danger.

residence

The place where someone lives. An individual whose **domicile** is England may have his residence in Manchester. He will be subject to the general **laws** of England but will be on the Manchester electoral roll, will be subject to Manchester **bye-laws** and will have his taxes collected locally.

residue

Property remaining after specific gifts have been made by **will.** The residue itself can be given to someone under the will. If it is not given, the residue is distributed according to the **intestacy** rules. *Residuary estate* is a long-winded way of saying residue.

res ipsa loquitur

[Latin: the thing speaks for itself] A catchphrase used in **negligence actions** and elsewhere by **lawyers.** If a car driven by

Jones runs off the road and into a wall, it can be assumed, in the absence of other **evidence,** that Jones was negligent in his driving: the thing speaks for itself. Intimacy with the phrase leads lawyers to speak of a *res ipsa case,* a *resipsy* and *RIL.*

res noviter

[Latin: short for 'a matter newly coming to knowledge'] In Scots **civil law,** a **plea** that new **evidence** has come to light which could not have been found at the time of the original **court** hearing. If successful, the plea could lead to a **decree** being set aside.

res judicata

[Latin: matter decided] The rule that a **court** will normally refuse to consider the same **case** twice, otherwise **litigation** would be unending. It does not preclude an **appeal.**

respondent

The **defender** in an **appeal** or **petition** to the **courts.**

rest, residue and remainder

These three r's are all Old French for the same thing—the leftovers. Thinking lawyers use **residue.**

restitution

The return of **property** to the rightful owner.

restraint of trade

See **public policy.**

restrictive covenant

An obligation in a **deed** which seeks to restrict the owner's rights. It may, for example, seek to prevent certain kinds of business being carried on on the **land.**

retrospective legislation

A new **law** that acts upon old matters, for example by making illegal something that was previously legal. Rare in English and Scots law.

return day

The date specified in a **summons** for the **hearing**. In Scotland, the day on which the summons must be returned to court in a **summary cause** or small debts claim.

rights of audience

The right of **solicitors** and **barristers** to argue a **case** in **court**. Under the Courts and Legal Services Act 1990, solicitors gained the right to argue cases in the higher courts, without briefing barristers.

right of first refusal

A right which long leaseholders and other **tenants** of privately owned blocks of flats have if their **landlord** is considering disposing of the **property** containing the flats. The landlord (with certain exceptions) must give them the right to buy their flats and tell them the price and the other main terms. If the tenants refuse the offer, the landlord may usually sell to anyone within a year provided he or she offers the same property on the same terms and at no lower price.

right of way

The right to pass over another individual's **land** without trespassing. There are three main types:

1 a public right which anyone can use;

2 a right conferred by **licence,** which may be personal to one individual or a few;

3 an **easement** which benefits owners of a particular piece of land.

See **footpath.**

right to buy

The right of **secure tenants** to buy the home they live in and obtain a **mortgage** from their **landlord.** Most secure tenants of district councils, London borough councils, new town development corporations, and non-charitable **housing associations** can exercise the right to buy.

right to silence

The right of someone on trial or charged with an **offence** to remain silent or refuse to give a **statement**. This cannot usually be held against him or her, though in a few instances it can—for example, in certain Department of Trade and **fraud** investigations, a suspect must answer questions otherwise silence will be incriminating. Someone who maintains silence during trial cannot bring forward at **appeal** matters which he or she could have raised at the trial. The right to silence in Northern Ireland trials was abolished in 1988 and the Home Secretary said it would soon be curtailed on the mainland.

riot

The use or threat of violence for a common purpose by 12 or more people together. It is punishable by up to 10 years in prison. Owners of **property** destroyed or stolen in a riot are entitled to **compensation** out of public money.

robbery

The use of force or fear in order to commit a **theft,** punishable by up to **life imprisonment.**

roup

In Scots, a public auction.

See **articles of roup.**

royal assent

The agreement of the Crown which converts a parliamentary bill into an **Act of Parliament.**

royalty

Payment for the right to use someone else's **property,** for example to reproduce copies of a work of art on postcards at a certain fee per card. Authors earn a very small royalty from publishers for each book sold.

Rule 43 prisoners

Rule 43 prisoners

Inmates kept apart from other prisoners for disciplinary reasons or because their **crimes,** eg sex **offences,** make them vulnerable to attack. They are also known as *nonces,* for no discernible reason. Separation is permitted by rule 43 of the prison rules.

S

The usual abbreviation when citing a section of a **law,** as in *s8 Vehicles (Excise) Act 1971* or, for more than one section, *ss.*

said, the

Legalese for a thing previously mentioned in a document. What exactly it refers back to is often unclear. Careful **lawyers** specify what they are referring back to: *the land mentioned in paragraph 12,* or *land A.*

The tradition of tagging *said* to people's names—*the said Arthur James*—is simply an archaic way of wasting paper.

Trainee **solicitors** are still given this sentence full of *saids* as a model of good practice for writing a **will:** *I revoke the gift of the said ordinary shares and I now give the said ordinary shares to the children of the said Gertrude Walters on the same terms and conditions as contained in my said will.* All four *saids* are redundant; the meaning of the words they are supposed to qualify was made clear at the start of the document.

sale of goods

A **contract** in which a seller transfers goods to a buyer for a price.

See **merchantable quality.**

salvage

Compensation paid to someone, the *salvor,* who saves a ship or its cargo from loss or damage at sea or in tidal waters. A salvor can claim an **award** in the **courts** if he or she acted voluntarily. Salvage may also be by prior agreement between the owner and salvor.

same, the

Legalese for something or someone previously mentioned in a document. The term usually means *it, them* or *this,* as in *Your* *client has committed a breach of contract and we have given him notice of same.* **Lawyers** who avoid legalese would use *the breach* or *it* instead. Regrettably *the same* appears at the start of every **Act of Parliament:** *Be it enacted by the Queen's most Excellent Majesty, by and with the advice and consent of the Lords Spiritual and Temporal, and Commons, in this present Parliament assembled, and by the authority of the same as follows.* As often happens, it is unclear here what *the same* refers to.

Sasines, Register of

/'seɪzɪnz/

A record of ownership of **heritage** in Scotland. It is open to public inspection in Edinburgh and takes the form of photocopied **title deeds**.

Sasine was originally a ceremony in which symbols of ownership were handed over on the **land** in front of **witnesses**.

See **Land Registry of Scotland**.

satisfactory quality

An implied condition in sales of goods which is likely to displace merchantable quality during 1992 if government proposals go through Parliament. It combines three ideas: goods must be (a) fit for purpose; (b) free from minor defects; (c) safe, durable and of appropriate appearance and finish.

save harmless

To protect against loss; indemnify. Sometimes found in quaintly worded declarations: *I promise to indemnify and save the council harmless in respect of this matter.*

scandalizing the judiciary

The offence under English law of making rude remarks about judges. Prosecutions are rare, though rude remarks are plentiful.

See **contempt of court**.

schedule

An appendix to a **law** or legal document which adds points of detail to the main part.

seal

Usually, wax impressed with a design and attached as a mark of authenticity to formal documents. Seals may also be produced by rubber stamps impressed on a document. The Great Seal, held by the Lord Chancellor, is used for sealing writs to summon Parliament, to seal treaties with foreign states, and to seal Acts of Parliament.

search warrant

See **Anton Piller; power of search.**

section 8 orders

In England and Wales, **court** orders made in any family proceedings, including adoption, under the Children Act 1989. They include:

1 residence orders, making arrangements about with whom **children** will live;

2 specific issues orders, dealing with any specific matter concerning **parental responsibility;**

3 contact orders, which require someone with whom a child lives to allow the child to visit or stay with the individual named in the order;

4 prohibited steps orders, which prevent parents who are exercising their parental responsibility from doing the things specified in the order, unless the court agrees.

Courts cannot make section 8 orders (except residence orders) concerning **children in care,** nor can such orders normally be made concerning any child over 16.

See **care order; child assessment order; emergency protection order; supervision order.**

Securities and Investment Board (SIB)

A **limited liability company** set up under the Financial Services Act 1986 which seeks to ensure that investment advisers are reputable, competent and solvent. It is an **offence** to do most kinds of investment business without SIB authorization; **contracts** made by unauthorized advisers may be unenforceable and investors who suffer loss may be able to get **compensation**.

secure tenant

A **tenant** or licensee who can only be moved out against his or her will by means of a **court** order for possession. To get such an order the **landlord** must satisfy the court that there is a good reason, such as non-payment of **rent,** breaking a **condition** of the tenancy, causing damage or getting the tenancy by false **statements**. Most tenants of district councils, London boroughs and **housing associations** are secure tenants.

On the death of a secure tenant, the tenancy passes to the **marriage** partner if he or she has been living there, or else to any close relative who has been living there for at least a year before the tenant's death. The automatic right of succession does not apply if the tenant had already been a successor after 3 October 1980, though many landlords will allow succession.

If you have a joint tenancy, it will pass to your **joint tenant** if you die, but there is no automatic right to succession after that.

See **assured tenancy; right to buy.**

security of tenure

Legal protection to **tenants** which restricts **landlords'** rights to retake possession. The extent of protection depends on the terms of the tenancy agreement and the type of tenancy. In general, residential tenants have the most protection.

See **assured tenancy; assured shorthold tenancy; regulated tenant; secure tenant.**

sedition

Attempts to incite people, by speech or writing, to violent and disorderly conduct with the aim of overthrowing the established order or government. This is a **common law offence** applying in particular to arousing hatred and contempt for the sovereign or her successors, the government and the administration of **justice**. Charges of sedition are rare.

seisin

/'si:zɪn/

Possession of a **freehold.** Now a rare term, as *possession* is enough for modern purposes, leading to the gradual death of such terms as *disseisin* and *seised in his demesne as of fee* which, a legal dictionary helpfully explains, means *a tenant in fee simple of his corporeal hereditament.* The verb *seise,* originally meaning to be put into legal possession, is gaining some ground outside the **law:** the company director becomes *seised* of the need for action if sales start to slide.

self defence

See **reasonable force.**

sending distressing letters

An **offence,** punishable by a **fine,** of sending someone a letter or other thing which bears an indecent, grossly offensive or threatening message, or false information known to the sender to be false, with the aim of causing distress or anxiety. It is also an offence to send someone an indecent or grossly offensive article without any message at all.

senior partner

One of the chiefs in a firm of **solicitors;** someone to resort to if the firm bungles your **case** or overcharges you.

sentence

A **court's judgment** on someone **guilty** of a **crime.** Before sentence, the **prosecution** must give the **judge** or **magistrate** information about the **accused's** *antecedents,* meaning criminal record, education, home circumstances etc. There may also be reports from specialists such as doctors, probation officers etc. The **defence** can then make a **plea in mitigation** of the sentence. The court may defer sentence until specialist reports are ready or for other reasons. Sentence is given in open court and usually in the accused's presence. The trial court can alter the sentence within 28 days if the judge changes his or her mind. The accused normally has a right of **appeal** to a higher court. The prosecution can appeal against the leniency of a **Crown Court** sentence. There are many types of sentence, including:

1 **fine**—a money penalty;

2 **community service** order—the offender must do a set amount of work for the public good;

3 confiscation order—the profits of crime may be seized;

4 **absolute discharge**—the individual is guilty but goes free without punishment (a *conditional discharge* has the same effect, but conditions are attached);

5 suspended—a prison term comes into force if the accused re-offends;

6 concurrent—a prison term to run parallel with another one;

7 consecutive—a prison term to run after another one.

sentence length

The distance between full stops in a legal document; often so great that the reader cannot understand the meaning easily. A **reasonable** average sentence length in a legal document or letter to a client is 15–20 words. Non-lawyers often assume that long sentences stem from a rule against punctuation in legal documents; even some **lawyers** believe this. There is no such rule. **Statutes** as far back as Magna Carta have been punctuated, and modern **laws** use a full range of punctuation as an aid to meaning.

separation of powers

A political doctrine associated with the 18th century philosopher Montesquieu. It argues that, to avoid tyranny, the three branches of government (law-making, administration, and judiciary) should be separated as far as possible, their relationships governed by checks and balances. The US Constitution is a practical example of an attempt to separate powers. Parliamentary systems like the UK's do not have a complete separation as the heads of administration (government ministers) sit in **Parliament,** the law-making body. The **Lord Chancellor** is the head of the judiciary but sits in the Lords and the Cabinet, having been appointed by the Crown on the advice of the prime minister. Nonetheless, our judiciary claims independence from the government of the day.

sequestration

1 In England and Wales, a **court** order in the form of a **writ** ordering commissioners to seize control of someone's **property,** perhaps because of disobedience of a court order.

2 In Scotland, a formal court process by which the bankrupt's property is taken, placed in the hands of a **trustee,** and distributed among **creditors**.

serious arrestable offence

See **arrest**.

Serious Fraud Office (SFO)

A body under the control of the **Attorney General** which investigates and prosecutes complex **frauds**.

service

The delivery of a document relating to **court** proceedings, such as a **writ** or **summons**. If a **litigant** has given an address for service, service may be by leaving the document at that address. **Personal service** means leaving the document with the litigant, having told him or her of its contents; it is not necessary to thrust it into his hand or touch him with it.

Substituted service means the service of documents other than by personal service. This may take the form of service by letter or public advertisement. It can be used, under court order, if a **defendant** is evading personal service.

service tenancy

A tenancy where the **tenant** is an employee of the **landlord** and the premises were let as a condition of the employment. The landlord needs a **court** order to regain possession after the employment has finished.

servient tenement
See **servitude.**

servitude
A right that benefits one area of **land** and in so doing burdens another in different ownership. The land getting the benefit is called the **dominant tenement,** the other is the **servient tenement.** For example, the owner of the dominant may have a right of access across the servient, or water from the dominant may lawfully run over the servient.

set-off
A **debtor's** right to have a money debt reduced by the amount that he or she claims the **creditor** owes in return.

setting aside
A **court** order cancelling a **judgment** or step.

settlement
1 The disposing of **property** by **deed** or **will,** under which **trusts** are created.

2 In Scotland, the day on which the **title** to a purchased property is handed over in return for payment.

several
See **joint and several.**

severance pay
Money which employees have a right to, in some circumstances, when their **contract** ends. An employee dismissed before the end of a fixed-term contract can claim money in lieu of the remainder of the contract, provided the employer was not entitled to dismiss. The most common form of severance pay is *in lieu of notice* if too little **notice** is given.

sex change

A change in someone's sexual characteristics by surgery or hormones. Some European countries allow transsexuals to marry after their sex change, but the European Court of Human Rights has ruled that British **law** cannot be compelled to follow their example. Transsexuals can, however, obtain a passport in their new sex.

sex discrimination

Discrimination in employment because of someone's sex: unlawful under the Equal Pay Act 1970 (EPA), the Sex Discrimination Acts of 1975 and 1986 (SDAs) and **European Community law**. Under the SDAs, discrimination in employment on the grounds of marital status is also unlawful. Under the EPA, men and women in the same employment must receive pay at the same rate for broadly similar work or work rated as equivalent or of equal value. The SDAs prohibit discrimination when offering an employment **contract** and offering promotion, and prohibit victimization of someone claiming discrimination. Someone who is discriminated against may bring a **civil case** for damages. Certain cases may be supported by the watchdog in this area, the Equal Opportunities Commission.

sexual intercourse

The penetration of the vagina by the penis. Formerly described in genteel questioning of a **witness** as *having connection,* as in *did you have connection with the accused?*

Another courtroom euphemism, with potentially more serious consequences, was *criminal conversation,* shortened to *crim. con.* This meant committing adultery with someone's wife and was regarded until 1857 as an **offence** against the husband's **property**.

shall

A word intended in legal writing to express obligation. It has become controversial in the battle between traditional legal writers and the modernists. Traditionalists believe the word is well understood and widely accepted as expressing legally binding force: *By this agreement, the landlord shall let and the tenant shall rent the premises.* The modernists say that ordinary folk regard *shall* as equivalent to *will*—the future tense. To express obligation, they prefer *must* or the present tense as being clearer and just as legally effective: *By this agreement, the landlord lets the premises and the tenant rents them.*

In British **Acts of Parliament,** *shall* is still used, whereas in new laws in Australia and Canada, *must* is slowly gaining ground.

In Britain many credit card and bank card conditions now use a combination of *must* and the present tense.

The word *may,* as in *the landlord may require the tenant to hand over the keys,* suggests that the **landlord** has discretion whether to do so or not.

sheriff

1 In England and Wales, the principal Crown officer in a county.

2 In Scotland, a **judge** in the **sheriff court**. The senior **judge** in a sheriffdom is the sheriff principal.

Sheriff court

In Scotland, an important lower **court** with wide jurisdiction in civil and criminal matters. It can deal with claims of unlimited value but not serious **crimes** like **murder** and **rape**. In **civil cases,** appeals against the court's decisions are usually heard by the **Inner House** of the **Court of Session**. In **criminal cases,** appeals are heard only by the High Court of Justiciary.

shew

The old form of the verb *show,* extinct in modern English except among **lawyers**.

shoplifting

Theft of goods from a shop without paying for them. To obtain a conviction it is necessary not only to prove that the goods were taken but that the **accused** intended to take them without paying—sometimes the accused can prove that he or she simply made a mistake or became confused.

See **mens rea.**

signature

The signing of a legal document. You are bound by what you sign, whether or not you read the document, unless you can prove **fraud,** illegality, **undue influence** or **misrepresentation.**

situate

Legalese for *at* or *situated,* as in *the land situate and known as 68 Smith Street, Anytown.* This just means *the land at 68 Smith Street, Anytown.*

slander

Defamation by word of mouth, although broadcast defamation is classed as **libel.** Slander might be the false allegation of unfitness for a job, incompetence or criminal behaviour (though **statements** to the police, in **court** and in **Parliament** are privileged). Someone bringing a **civil action** for slander must show actual loss, for example loss of a **contract.** By its nature slander tends to be transient and the evidence unreliable. Since the cost of **cases** is high and winnings are usually low, few people bother to **sue.** An exchange of irate **solicitors'** letters is the furthest most actions go. **Legal aid** is not available to bring or defend proceedings.

See **privilege.**

slander of goods

In **civil law,** a false statement, made maliciously, pointing out a specific defect in a trader's goods.

small claims

Civil actions in the **county courts** for claims up to £1,000, often concerning consumers' disputes with traders. **Cases** tend to be settled in a less formal way and quicker than other county court matters, using an **arbitration** procedure before a **district judge.** Many people act as their own **lawyers,** though they can use a friend, **solicitor** or perhaps a citizens advice bureau worker. It is unusual for the loser to be ordered to pay the other side's costs, so the **litigant** risks only the **court** and **witness** fees (about £50–75) if he or she loses. The small claims procedure has not entirely dispensed with conventional court practices, and it can be quite daunting for an unrepresented litigant to present a case and be cross-examined by an opponent's **solicitor**. But it can also be good fun and a reasonably cheap way of having your day in court. With a good case you are likely to win against even a well represented opponent. Your problem then is how to enforce the court **judgment** if the loser refuses to pay up—the court's enforcement system is often slow and ineffective.

small print

The term often used for the fine details of an agreement, although it could refer to the size of the typeset text itself.

There is no legal minimum size of type for consumer agreements such as sales on credit, but most such agreements must by **law** be 'easily legible'—this is not defined, so it could mean almost anything. A **provision** hidden in tiny type or printed in nearly invisible ink might be difficult for a company to enforce.

There is no legal standard for the clarity of language in an agreement—the law does not say that agreements must be understandable to the average individual who is likely to sign them. Laws governing the clarity of language and layout of certain consumer agreements exist in many states in the USA.

See **Clarity; sentence, length of.**

soliciting

The **offence** by a prostitute of trying to attract **clients** in a street or public place.

See **kerb crawling.**

solicitor

[Latin *sollicitare*: to stir up] A **lawyer,** known formally in the UK as a Solicitor of the Supreme Court, whose responsibilities include giving legal advice to **clients**. Solicitors have a **fiduciary relationship** with their **clients,** including the maintaining of confidentiality towards a client's affairs. Solicitors can be removed from the roll of Supreme Court solicitors at their request or *struck off* for misconduct.

On the face of it, the relationship between a client and his (or her) solicitor is like that between a prime minister and a technical adviser. You, the client, are the prime minister. You give the instructions, pay the adviser's fees, and take the rap if things go wrong. The solicitor is your technical adviser. He (or she) suggests possible courses of action and explains the **law**. He writes letters for you and may attend meetings on your behalf, as when representing you in **court** or negotiating with the other side.

Few clients view the relationship in this way. Knowing little of the law, they consider themselves inferior to their adviser. They meet him on foreign territory, his office, where he sits behind a desk surrounded by his papers and telephones while being attended by his servants. And to add to their feeling of inferiority as mere clients, they are probably paying him more in an hour than they earn in a day. It is difficult—for both sides—to handle this relationship successfully.

Nor is choosing the right solicitor easy. Recommendations from satisfied customers are a good guide, so it makes sense to tap the experiences of your friends or colleagues. Failing that, your **trade union** or employer may be able to help. Yellow Pages is a last resort as the adverts give little useful information and are written by the solicitors themselves. (In Scotland, the Law Society of Scotland will provide a list of solicitors who deal with a specific area of law.)

Solicitors do some things better than others. Some are better at routine work like **wills** and conveyancing. A small rural practice may not be able to handle a big **case** involving complex **litigation**. It is sensible to 'view the goods' by meeting several solicitors and discussing your problem with them. You should say quite openly that you are talking to several to see who suits you best. Those who refuse to see you on this basis are best avoided; if they don't have time for you now, they won't later. Go armed with a written list of points about your problem—this is good policy whenever you meet your solicitor.

Then consider whether the solicitor met your needs. Was he a good listener? Did he ask intelligent questions and grasp the problem quickly? Did he have time for you? Did he divert his phone calls so that you had his undivided attention? Or was he a pompous ass?

When you have engaged a solicitor, you have a right to expect a good standard of customer care. Your phone calls should be acted upon with **reasonable** speed. Obviously a busy solicitor cannot drop everything just to handle your case, but he should stay on top of it. If an absent solicitor fails to return your call, it may simply be to save you money since you pay for every letter and call. Even so, if there is nothing to report, his office should tell you as a matter of courtesy.

A knowledgeable solicitor should not be running to get a **barrister's opinion** on minor details of the case; this will cost you money. On the other hand, barristers will be cheaper than your solicitor for some things, like drafting **pleadings**. You can ask for an advance estimate of the cost of most legal work, though in some kinds of litigation the costs are difficult to gauge in advance.

Keep a brief note of what is said in every phone call and meeting with your solicitor, and when the conversations occurred. This provides a useful record if he botches the case or overcharges you.

Your solicitor needs to be good at drafting clear and effective letters and other documents without resorting to hereofs, **whereofs** and **thereofs**. If you cannot make sense of what he writes, ask for an explanation in clear English. The vast majority of complaints to the **Solicitors Complaints Bureau** arise from solicitors' failure to communicate clearly and quickly with their clients. A considerate solicitor will keep you informed of what has happened, how the situation stands, and what you can expect next.

If a solicitor's work is below par, you can change to a different one. If you are on **legal aid,** you will need to get the Legal Aid Fund's permission to change.

See **BS5750; file, client's.**

Solicitors Complaints Bureau

An organization set up by the **Law Society**—the solicitors' professional body—which seeks to ensure that **solicitors** observe proper standards of behaviour when dealing with **clients** and other solicitors. Clients may complain to the bureau, but only after they have complained to the solicitor and the solicitor's **senior partner,** if there is one. The sort of problem that the bureau investigates includes:

1 delay in answering letters or enquiries;

2 delay in dealing with your **case;**

3 failure to deal with your money properly;

4 acting in the same case for you and for others where your **interests** conflict with those of the other clients;

5 dishonesty or deception;

6 incompetent or shoddy work.

The bureau can order a solicitor to reduce a bill or put right shoddy work. It can award up to £1,000 **compensation,** but not for **negligence.** If your solicitor has made a mistake which has cost you money or some other loss, the bureau will help you find another solicitor who will give a free initial interview to help you decide whether to pursue a legal **action** for negligence. (The scheme is not available to limited companies.) It may be possible to settle any claim by **arbitration** if you and the original solicitor agree.

If you have difficulty writing out your complaint, the bureau may be able to ask another solicitor to meet you and discuss the case.

It is also possible to complain to the bureau about conduct by solicitors acting for your opponents. But solicitors have a duty to do their best for their clients and are entitled to act on what their clients say. So if their clients tell them a pack of lies, it's not the solicitors' responsibility to check the **facts**—as long as they act legally and properly, they're in the clear. If you feel that your opponent's solicitor has acted illegally or improperly, tell your own solicitors. If they agree, they must report it to the bureau.

Complaints about Scottish solicitors are dealt with by the Law Society of Scotland.

See **remuneration certificate; taxation of costs.**

Solicitors Disciplinary Tribunal
In England and Wales, a disciplinary body set up by **Parliament**. It can strike a **solicitor** off the Roll of Solicitors, suspend him or her from practice or impose a fine or reprimand.

sorry
An expression of regret rarely employed by the judiciary even after the most ghastly **miscarriages of justice**.

Special Branch
Police officers attached to each regional police force who gather information about threats to public order, subversion, the IRA etc.

special constables
The 16 000 unpaid part-time volunteer members of the special constabulary who have all the powers of regular police officers. They tend to deal with 'soft' duties such as traffic and public order, but are increasingly deployed in tougher roles. Their only distinguishing mark from the regulars are the letters SC above their identity numbers.

special hospital
A hospital such as Broadmoor, Rampton or Carstairs for people suffering from mental disorder who need to be detained under special security.

special verdict
See **insanity**.

specific performance
See **performance**.

specimen of blood, breath or urine
See **breathalyser**.

speeding

> The **offence** of driving a motor vehicle at a speed above the limit permitted for the road and the kind of vehicle, whether or not this caused danger to others.
>
> See **strict liability**.

spent conviction

> A criminal conviction which, after a set number of years, can be treated in civil proceedings as if it had never existed. The period is known as the *rehabilitation period* and it varies with the seriousness of the **offence**. A spent conviction need not be disclosed when applying for jobs, though there are exceptions in certain occupations.

standard of proof

> See **civil cases; criminal law**.

stare decisis

> [Latin: to stand by things decided] A maxim which underpins the doctrine of **precedent**.

statement

> 1 A written and signed record of someone's knowledge of a particular matter.
>
> 2 A statement of special educational needs under the Education Act. If a **child** has learning difficulties, a statement will be agreed between the parents, education authority and the school. It will set out what extra help will be provided to meet the needs. Hence schools speak of having a child *statemented*.

statement of claim

> In a **civil case** started by a **High Court writ**, a **pleading** stating the **plaintiff's** allegations against the **defendant** and the **relief** he or she seeks.

statute

In the UK, an **Act of Parliament**. This becomes part of the written body of **law**. Hence the term *statute book,* a mythical single volume.

Statute of Pleading

A **law** of 1362 which said that **court** proceedings must be 'pleaded, shewed, defended, answered, debated and judged in the English tongue' because **litigants** could not understand the French being used by **lawyers** and **judges**. Written records continued to be in Latin as did **writs,** though they were available in French (not English) translation. Since **statutes** were written in French (including the statute about using English!) until the end of the 15th century, and since there were no English law books, French and Latin continued to be regularly used in court proceedings until 1650. **Parliament** then passed an 'Act for turning the Books of the Law, and all Proces and Proceedings in Courts of Justice, into English.' Many **barristers** hated the idea and the Restoration of 1660 tried to reinstate the old ways. But English's time had come. Within a few decades, even without a statute, English had asserted itself as the normal language of the **courts** and legal reporting; this finally became statutory in 1731. Lawyers then got into a tangle trying to translate some of their Latin **terms of art** into English, so an amendment of 1733 permitted their retention and use. This is why Latin words still litter the language of the modern law, and why one may still be lawfully served with writs of **certiorari, mandamus, habeas corpus, fieri facias** and the rest.

See **franglais.**

statutory body

A body set up by Act of Parliament to perform some function that the state considers desirable.

statutory instrument

A way of publishing **delegated legislation.**

stay

A **court** order suspending some step that would otherwise be taken.

stay of execution

A **court** order suspending the effect of another court order.

stipendiary magistrate ('stipe')

In England and Wales, a salaried and legally qualified **magistrate**. Such magistrates may sit alone when trying **cases,** unlike lay magistrates. There are only about 60 in England and Wales, of whom about 40 work in London. Stipendiaries were created during the 18th century in response to widespread corruption among the lay magistrates in London's 'poor courts', where **justice** could be bought.

strict liability

A principle which removes the need, in some **cases,** to prove negligence or intention by wrongdoers; it is enough to prove that their actions caused the injury or problem. Many motoring **offences,** like **speeding,** are strict liability offences. The motorist went through the red light; whether he intended to is irrelevant. The principle does not apply in most kinds of **civil case.** For example, someone suing a company responsible for pollution which damages their health would have to prove that the company had acted negligently or breached a legal duty before **damages** could be won—this is very difficult to do.

See **no-fault compensation; nuisance.**

strike

Employees' refusal to work in an effort to win better terms and conditions of employment or against certain actions of employers. A **trade union** may only call a lawful strike if it has held a secret ballot and the majority agree to join in. Employees dismissed for striking can claim **unfair dismissal** in some circumstances.

See **picketing; trade dispute; trade union.**

striking off
See **Solicitors Disciplinary Tribunal.**

structured settlement
The payment of **damages** in stages instead of as a lump sum in personal injury **cases. Courts** have begun to impose these settlements if a victim needs long term care or if there is a risk of a lump sum being squandered. There may be tax advantages to both sides.

subjects
In Scots law, **legalese** for *heritable property* (ie **land** and buildings) though it can also mean **moveable property.**

sub judice
[Latin: under law] A rule restricting the discussion or reporting of matters related to legal proceedings. The aim is to avoid prejudging the **case** or influencing a **jury. Lawyers** are divided on whether to pronounce the word with a hard or soft c.

subpoena
[Latin: under penalty] A **court** order telling someone to appear in court on a certain day to give **evidence** or to produce documents needed as evidence.

substituted service
See **service.**

sue
To make a **claim** in the **civil courts.**

suicide
Intentional killing of oneself; this is not an **offence** though there is an offence of helping someone to commit suicide. In a *suicide pact,* where two people decide to take their lives together, if the one who kills the other survives, he or she may be **guilty** of **manslaughter** not **murder.**

suit

A **civil court claim.**

summary cause

In Scotland, a **civil claim** for less than £1 500. Such cases are heard in the **sheriff court** using a simplified procedure.

summary offence

An **offence** that can only be tried in a **magistrates' court** or, in Scotland, the **sheriff court**. Hence *summary conviction* and *summary trial.*

See **magistrates.**

summing-up

See **jury.**

summons

A **court** order summoning someone to appear in certain courts at a certain place and time.

supervision order

A **court** order putting a **child** under the supervision of the **local authority,** welfare officer or probation officer. The supervisor has a duty to advise, assist and befriend.

surprise

An unexpected event or **fact** that puts a **litigant** at a disadvantage in the courtroom. Pre-trial procedures like the **disclosure of documents** by both **parties** are designed to prevent surprise which can cause a **judge** to allow a **case** to be adjourned.

suspended sentence

See **sentence.**

sustain

In Scots law, to uphold a **plea-in-law.**

See **interlocutor; repel.**

T

talaq

An Islamic **divorce,** usually performed by the husband saying to his wife *I divorce you* three times informally or in **court**. It has effect in England and Wales only if done outside the UK, Channel Islands and Isle of Man.

taxation of costs

This is nothing to do with tax in the **Inland Revenue** sense. It is the method by which a **court** official decides the amount of **costs** payable by one side to the other or by a **client** to a **solicitor.** In London, taxation is done by *taxing masters;* outside London, by *district registrars.* The method can be used whether or not court proceedings have been issued.

If you think your solicitor's bill is too high you can apply for it to be taxed. You and your solicitor can both tell the court what you think about the bill. If the bill is cut by less than a fifth, you will normally have to pay for the costs of taxation as well as the bill. If the bill is cut by more than a fifth, your solicitor will have to pay them. You will then have to pay the bill as reduced. There are **time limits** on applying for taxation; it is safest to apply within a month of receiving the bill and without having paid it.

TDA

Police acronym for *Taking and Driving Away:* a car **theft offence.**

telephone tapping

Secretly listening to phone conversations by manual or mechanical interception of calls. It is only lawful when authorized by the **Home Office** or Scottish Office, which in 1990 authorized 515 interception **warrants.** These permitted phone conversations to be secretly taped and transcribed or mail to be intercepted. Each warrant may apply to a whole organization, so the number of warrants does not give a clear picture of the extent of interception. Most of the warrants relate to drug trafficking and terrorism, with relatively few in pursuit of political subversives. By the mid-1990s, telephone tapping will be fully computerized at a high security listening post in Oswestry. In France, police unions estimate there are between 10 000 and 50 000 official and unofficial taps every year.

tenant

An individual or business who holds **land** or other **property** under a **lease** or tenancy from a **landlord** for an agreed period in return for **rent**.

See **assured tenant; assured shorthold tenant; regulated tenant; secure tenant.**

tenement

A building containing separate **properties** or flats. Rules known as the *law of tenement* regulate the rights and duties of the owners in Scotland.

term

1 A period of time. For example, a **lease** may run for a term of 10 years.

2 A **provision** which forms part of a **contract**. See **condition**.

term of years absolute

Legalese for **leasehold**.

terms of art

Technical words and phrases with specific meanings. **Law,** like many professions, industries and games, uses terms of art which provide useful shorthand for practitioners. They include **tort, mandamus, plaintiff, habeas corpus, negligence.**

See **legalese.**

testament
A **will**.

See **last will and testament**.

testamentary capacity
The ability to make a legally valid **will**. People under 18 (unless on active service with the armed services) and mental patients cannot make a valid will, nor can people who do not understand what they are doing at the time. In Scotland, children of 12 and over have full testamentary capacity.

testamentary expenses
The expenses of administering a **deceased's estate**.

testate
Leaving a legally valid **will** on death.

See **intestacy**.

testator
[Latin *testari:* to make a will] A **will** maker; the female of the species is a *testatrix.*

test case
A **case** used to test a legal principle which can then be applied to other cases.

theft
See **dishonesty**.

thereafter
Afterwards; from that time on; after.

thereby
By that means; thus. For example *The contract thereby created will immediately end.* The word is antiquated and often redundant.

thereof

Legalese for *of it* or *concerning that.*

thereto

Legalese for *to that* or *to it.* For example *The schedule is attached thereto.* Modern English would use *The schedule is attached to it.*

third party

Someone other than one of the **parties** to a **contract.** For example, in a motor insurance policy, the *first party* is the insured, the *second party* is the insurance company, and the third party is anyone whom the insured injures in a road accident.

threatening behaviour

In England and Wales, the **offence** of using threatening, insulting or abusive words to someone with the aim of causing that individual to fear imminent violence. The same offence applies to the written word but does not apply within someone's home. In Scotland, threats may be criminal and result in a **breach of the peace,** for example.

thereupon

At that time or *just afterwards.*

time limit

See **limitation of action**.

timeous

Scots for *punctual* or *in due time.*

timeshare

A limited **interest** in **land,** perhaps for one week a year for 99 years.

title

Someone's right of ownership to **property.** If a **person** is said to have good **title,** their **interest** in the property can be proven.

title deeds

See **land certificate.**

to have and to hold

A term used in **leases** to indicate possession, but more famously in The Book of Common Prayer's **marriage** ceremony. The words *have* and *hold* are synonyms in Old English; such tautology is common in **law** language (see **null and void**). In modern law, either *have* or *hold* would do the job.

Tomlin order

In England and Wales, a form of **court** order which brings a civil **action** to a close out of court by consent between the **parties** on terms attached to the order. The particular kind of order is based on a **Practice Direction** issued by Mr Justice Tomlin in 1927.

tort

[from Old French through Latin: twisted or crooked] A wrong, actionable in the **civil courts**. Torts include **negligence,** trespass, **nuisance, libel** and **passing off,** but not breach of **contract.** The usual remedies are damages, an injunction or both. Alternatively the **plaintiff** can call for an **account of profits** arising from the wrong, and demand to receive payment of them. The analogous term in Scots law is **delict.**

See **trespassers will be prosecuted.**

tort-feasor

A wrongdoer under **civil law.**

totting up

The process of adding up **offences** endorsed on a **driving licence** so that a **court** may order disqualification from driving when a certain limit has been reached.

Trade Descriptions Act 1968

The Act which makes it an **offence** to falsely describe goods during their sale in the course of business. The false description may concern quantity, size, fitness for purpose, price and method of manufacture. It may be *direct,* as in turning back a car's mileometer, or *indirect,* as in painting over a patch of rust.

See **fit for purpose.**

trade dispute

A dispute between workers and their employer or between workers and workers concerning one or more of the following: employment terms and conditions; taking on, not taking on, suspending or dismissing a worker; allocation of duties among workers; discipline; **trade union** membership or non-membership; facilities for trade union officials; machinery for negotiation or consultation.

See **picketing; strike.**

trade mark

A distinctive symbol, perhaps consisting of words or a design, which identifies a particular trader's products. A trade mark can be protected through registration at the Patent Office on the Register of Trade Marks. Protection lasts initially for 7 years but is renewable. The trader can license the use of the mark, with the Registrar's permission. If anyone else uses the mark or creates a mark which is similar to it, the trader can **sue** in **tort.** Well known trade marks include *Elastoplast, Portakabin, Nabisco* and *Gazza.*

See **patent.**

trade secret

Information about a product or process belonging to a business which, if disclosed, could harm the business. Anyone who threatens to disclose a trade secret with which they have been entrusted could become subject to an **injunction** to stop them.

trade union

An organization whose members are mainly workers and whose main aim includes the improvement of pay and working conditions by collective bargaining with employers. The conduct of unions is governed by their own rule books, the Trade Union Act 1984 and the Employment Act 1988. These Acts say that:

1 members may not be unjustifiably disciplined, for example, for not going on strike;

2 secret ballots must be held for **elections** to union executive committees and before **strike** actions, work-to-rule etc;

3 union funds must not be used to pay members' fines for criminal **offences** or **contempt of court;**

4 union accounts must be open to members' inspection.

See **picketing; trade dispute.**

trainee solicitor

In England and Wales, someone training to be a solicitor, usually by working in a solicitor's office. He or she is *doing articles.* Formerly called an **articled clerk.**

treason

The **crime** of failing to pay proper allegiance to a government or monarch. The main forms of treason are:

1 conspiring or inciting to have the monarch killed;

2 making war against the monarch—insurrection in the UK;

3 giving aid or comfort to the monarch's enemies in wartime.

Disloyalty is essential to the crime—someone who commits treason must owe allegiance to the Crown—so a non-British subject could only commit treason if the acts were done while sheltering under the Crown's protection. In practice, treason is an improbable charge, even in wartime. The **penalty** for treason is death by hanging, a relatively pleasant and modern innovation brought in by the Forfeiture Act of 1870 which replaced burning (for women) and hanging, beheading and quartering (in that order) for men. This was itself a replacement for hanging and being disembowelled while alive, which was stopped in 1814.

treasure trove

Articles of gold and silver found hidden in a concealed place, the owner being unknown. It belongs to the Crown, though the finder is usually rewarded.

treasury devil

A **barrister** who represents the government in **court**.

treaty

An international written agreement between or among states. In the UK the monarch alone has the power to make treaties, acting on advice from government ministers.

tree preservation order

A local planning authority order preventing the felling of trees specified in the order.

trespassers will be prosecuted

In England and Wales, *trespass* means direct interference with a **property** by entering **land** without the owner's or **tenant's** consent, whether damage is caused or not, or taking goods without consent. This is usually a **tort** so a trespasser can be sued, though it is not usually worth it. The popular notice is therefore usually misleading.

It is a **crime** to use even **reasonable** force against a trespasser unless you are trying, for example, to get rid of squatters from your own home.

In 1986 the scope of *criminal trespass* became wider after public hysteria about New Age Travellers, branded by the then Home Secretary as 'medieval brigands'. The then prime minister said she would do 'anything I can to make life difficult for such things as hippy convoys.' What was done was to insert a clause in the Public Order Act 1986 which created a new police power. If two or more people are present on land, and a senior police officer reasonably believes they have entered as trespassers, that the occupier has asked them to leave and that they have a common purpose of living there, he will be able to ask them to leave the land if one of three tests is fulfilled: any

229

of the trespassers has (a) caused damage; (b) used threats or abuse to the occupier; or (c) brought between them 12 or more vehicles onto the land. The **penalty** is up to £1,000 fine or 3 months' jail.

In Scotland, trespass is any temporary intrusion on someone else's land without permission.

tribunal

An official body performing functions of a judicial nature. Tribunals often deal with matters where the citizen is in conflict with a government department. They tend to be specialized, dealing with such issues as employment rights, mental health and taxation. Someone dissatisfied with a tribunal decision may call for **judicial review**.

See **Employment Appeal Tribunal; industrial tribunal.**

trust

An arrangement in which a **person** (the *trustee*) holds **property** for the benefit of another (the *beneficiary*), under the terms of a **settlement** or **will** which binds the trustees.

The beneficiary cannot sell the property and may take only the interest or income from it during his lifetime. This is a way of keeping intact a capital sum until, for example, the beneficiary dies. At that point the property might revert to the **estate** of the will-maker and someone else would benefit under the terms of the will. Trusts have been widely used by the wealthy to avoid tax and to stop a spendthrift family member pauperizing his relatives by going on a spree with the family money.

A trustee must show a high standard of care to the beneficiaries and must not allow his or her own interests to conflict with the beneficiaries'. A trustee in breach of a trust is liable for the damage suffered.

See **remainder.**

trustee in bankruptcy

In England and Wales, a **person** who holds a bankrupt's assets for the benefit of the bankrupt's **creditors,** selling them and distributing the proceeds among those with valid **claims.** The trustee gives a public **notice** that someone is bankrupt and sets a *last day for receiving proofs*—the date by which creditors must submit proof of their claims.

See **bankruptcy.**

TWOC

Police slang for *Taking and driving away Without the Owner's Consent*: an **offence.**

U

uberrimae fidei
See **insurance policy**.

ultra vires
[Latin: beyond the powers] A phrase describing the actions of any body that exceeds the authority given to it by an **Act of Parliament, trust deed, memorandum of association,** rule book etc. A **local authority** which sends a gift to a group of foreign freedom fighters would be acting ultra vires, as might a body that disobeyed its own procedures. Among possible remedies are **injunction** and **certiorari**. Actions which are consistent with a body's powers are known as *intra vires*.

undischarged bankrupt
Someone who has been made bankrupt but has not yet received a **discharge order** from the **court**.

See **bankruptcy**.

undue influence
In **contract law,** improper pressure by one **person** on another in relation to a transaction. A **court** can set aside a gift or contract obtained by someone who has taken unfair advantage of another. In certain relationships, such as between a **solicitor** and **client** or religious leader and follower, undue influence is assumed to exist automatically, so in a court **case** the stronger party would have to prove that it had not been exercised.

unfair contract terms
Terms in a **contract** which seek to exclude or restrict the liability of a business to a consumer in a way which the Unfair Contract Terms Act 1977 prohibits or allows only so far as the terms are **reasonable**. The Act says that in a contract or **notice** a business:

1 may not exclude or restrict liability for **negligence** which results in death or personal injury;

2 may not exclude or restrict liability for other loss or damage resulting from negligence in a guarantee given with consumer goods;

3 may exclude or restrict liability (except for death or personal injury caused by negligence) so far as a **court** decides the exclusion is reasonable.

In a dispute it would be for the business to prove to the court that the exclusion or restriction was reasonable. The court would consider such things as what the **parties** knew of the circumstances when the contract was made, what were the relative strengths of the parties to the bargain, whether a discount was given to the buyer to sweeten the exclusion, and how easily the goods could have been got elsewhere without the exclusion.

Exclusion clauses relied on by film processing companies to avoid compensating customers for lost films have been set aside as unreasonable by the courts.

Notices in council car parks saying: 'The council accepts no liability to visitors for loss or damage to property however caused while on these premises' would be subject to a similar reasonableness test if a legal **action** arose.

unfair dismissal

The unjustifiable dismissal of an employee. Provided that an employee has at least two years' continuous service with the employer, and is under the normal retirement age for the job, he or she can claim unfair dismissal. Even if he or she has not fulfilled these conditions but has been dismissed for membership or non-membership of a **trade union,** he or she can claim unfair dismissal. A **case** for unfair dismissal must be started within 3 months of the effective date of dismissal (the last day of work if proper **notice** had been given). The **claim—** to an **industrial tribunal**—could be for getting back your old job, getting a new job with the firm if the need for your old job has disappeared, or **compensation.**

Certain dismissals are always unfair, including dismissal for trade union reasons, pregnancy, and sex and race discrimination.

See **racial discrimination; sex discrimination**.

unfit to plead

An **accused** who cannot be tried because of a disability such as mental illness.

unincorporated body

An association whose legal personality is identical to that of its members, who therefore do not enjoy limited liability. Unincorporated bodies include partnerships and clubs. In a club, the committee members or trustees would normally be liable for its debts.

See **corporation; limited liability company; person**.

United Kingdom

Scotland, Wales, England, and Northern Ireland together.

See **jurisdiction**.

unlawful sexual intercourse

Sexual intercourse with a girl under 16, a mentally defective woman, or occurring in any other sexual offence such as **rape, incest** etc.

unlawful wounding

See **wounding**.

unlimited company

A registered company whose members do not have limited liability. When such companies are wound up, **creditors** can call on the members' own assets to meet their claims. Unlimited companies do not have to reveal accounts to the Companies Registry.

See **limited liability company**.

unsecured creditor

Someone who has lent money without getting **security** for the loan.

See **secured creditor**.

unsolicited goods

Goods sent to a private consumer who did not ask for them. It is an **offence** to demand payment for them. The consumer may not destroy or damage them but can keep them if they are not collected within 6 months or within 30 days of asking for them to be collected.

V

v

Abbreviation for *versus,* used in the titles of legal **actions:** *Patel v Smith.*

vacant possession

A description applied to premises which are for sale or have been sold without being subject to any **lease.**

vendor

A seller. In the **Law Society's** standard **conveyancing** documents, the old fashioned *vendor* has been replaced by *seller.*

venereal disease

An infectious disease like gonorrhea or syphilis which is transmitted through sexual contact. A married man with a venereal disease is not entitled to insist on sex with his wife— this might be considered **rape** and would certainly give his wife grounds for **divorce.** If at the time of **marriage** a partner is suffering from a venereal disease and the other partner does not know it, the marriage can be annulled.

See **annulment.**

verbals

Remarks made by an **accused** in the presence of police officers, which can be written down and used as **evidence.**

verdict

[From Latin and French: truly said] A **jury's** finding in a trial.

See **perverse verdict.**

vest

To confer authority, legal rights or ownership of **land** on someone, as in: *The powers of the club are vested in the committee.*

veto

[Latin: I forbid] In **international law,** the right of a member of the United Nations Security Council to refuse to agree to a proposal, which then falls.

vexatious litigant

See **litigant.**

vicarious liability

[From Latin *vicarius*: a deputy] Legal liability which a **person** must bear for wrongs done by someone else. An employer may be vicariously liable for **offences** by employees during the course of their work, such as negligent driving. The employee also remains personally liable.

Victim Support

An organization which provides help and guidance to victims of **crime** through 400 schemes nationwide. The schemes are staffed mainly by volunteers and funded by the **Home Office** and **local authorities.**

video link

A closed circuit television system in a **court** building. **Children** under 14 can now give evidence by video link in some **Crown Courts,** so they do not have to face the **defendant, judge** or **barristers.** Currently the link is live, so children still have to attend court. Its use is restricted to serious cases of sex abuse and violence.

In all criminal cases screens are available at the court's discretion to give privacy to **witnesses** under the age of 18. This stems from a case in 1988 when Judge Thomas Pigot decided to allow a 13-year-old victim of sexual abuse to give her **evidence** from behind a screen. He also told barristers to take off their wigs and cleared the public gallery so that friends of the **accused** could not see her. Not all judges have taken similar steps. In 1991 a 16-year-old victim of a multiple **rape** had to give evidence in open court after a judge refused requests for a screen.

violent disorder

An **offence** of using or threatening to use violent conduct towards people or **property,** committed by three or more people acting together.

void

See **null and void.**

voidable contract

A **contract** which was valid when it was made, but can be set aside by a **court** perhaps because of a **misrepresentation** which induced someone to become a **party** to the contract, **undue influence** or **mistake.**

See **void contract.**

void contract

A **contract** that lacked any legal effect from the time it was made, perhaps because it was illegal, eg a contract to supply women for **prostitution,** or against **public policy,** eg certain kinds of **restraint of trade.** Some serious mistakes made at the time of entering a contract may make it void.

See **voidable contract.**

volenti

[From Latin *volenti non fit injuria*: to him who consents, no harm is done] A **defence** to a **claim** for **damages** which says that the injured **person** consented to the action. For example, a rugby player injured in a tackle cannot win damages because his voluntary participation in such a sport implies that he accepts the risks. But if the **court** decides that the tackle was deliberate and **reckless** foul play outside the rules of the game, he could win damages. Generally employees and rescuers fall outside the categories of people whom the courts regard as having voluntarily run the risk of accident.

voluntary arrangement

An agreement between a **debtor** (an individual or a business) and his or her **creditors** concerning the payment of debts under the Insolvency Act 1986.

voluntary liquidation

The winding-up of a company by a resolution of the members that the company should be wound up. It is classed either as:

1 a members' voluntary winding-up if the **directors** have made a **declaration** that the company can meet its debts; or

2 a creditors' voluntary winding-up if there is no such declaration or if the **liquidator** in a members' winding-up disagrees with the directors' view on the company's ability to pay its debts.

The directors' powers cease when the liquidator is appointed.

See **winding-up order.**

W

waive

To give up one's rights.

war crime

A violation of the **laws** and customs of war which amounts to a criminal act. This includes **murder,** ill-treatment of prisoners and civilian populations, plundering **property,** devastation of population centres not justified by military needs, persecution of civilians on political, religious or racial grounds, planning or waging a war of aggression or in violation of international treaties. **Prosecution** for war crimes is normally undertaken by the winners.

ward of court

1 A **child** under the care of a **guardian,** who has **parental responsibility** for the child under the general control of a **court.**

2 A child over whom a court has assumed parental responsibility under a *wardship order.*

warrant

A written document from a **magistrate** which authorizes the **arrest** of a suspect or the searching of **property**.

warrant sale

See **poinding.**

warranty

See **contract.**

war risks

Insurance risks arising from hostilities, rebellion, revolution and civil war. These are usually excluded from the cover given by **insurance policies.**

waste

An alteration of tenanted **property** by the **tenant's** actions or lack of them. Tenants are usually liable for the cost of reinstatement, though fair wear and tear is normally excluded.

wasting police time

The **offence** of making a false report to the police which causes them to investigate. It is punishable by **fine** or imprisonment.

wayleave

A **right of way** under, across or over **land,** for example for pipelines and cables.

wearing apparel

Legalese for *clothing,* as in *the trustee shall dispose of my wearing apparel.*

whencesoever

From whatever source.

whereas

An imprecise word which has any number of meanings including *on the contrary* (its meaning in popular speech and writing), *although* or *in view of the fact that.* It is often used in the preamble to a **contract:**

'Whereas James Smith owns two sheep and one goat. And whereas the **aforesaid** James Smith owns land at Spinney Meadow, Oxenford.'

Such usage breaks grammatical convention because the 'sentences' appear to be incomplete. Whereas seems to be functioning as a harrumph—a kind of ritual throat clearance—to get the document under way.

This use of whereas has found a modern home in the preambles to European Community directives, where it prefixes every **fact** that the law-makers have taken into account in framing the directive. Sometimes as many as 50 statements are whereased. It would be just as effective to say at the start: 'These facts have been taken into account' or 'Background' and then list the facts.

whereof

Legalese for *of which; of this.* For example *in witness whereof we sign the document* means *to witness this we sign the document.*

wherein

Legalese for *in which place; in which thing.*

whereupon

At which time.

White Book

1 A detailed reference work properly called *The Supreme Court Practice.* It describes the rules of practice and procedure in all the higher courts except the **House of Lords**.

2 In Scotland, the name given to the Scottish Law Directory.

wilful

Deliberate.

will

A document in which someone sets out how his or her **property** (the **estate**) is to be distributed to beneficiaries after death. To be valid, a will must comply with certain requirements. For example, it must be signed in front of two **witnesses** present at the same time, and the **testator** (will-maker) must have **testamentary capacity,** in other words, know what he or she is doing and have reached an age at which he or she is permitted to make a will.

A dependant, such as a **marriage** partner, can expect to get **reasonable** financial provision under a will, and can apply to the **court** if this does not happen.

A will can be amended by the testator adding a **codicil** or striking out unwanted words. It can be revoked by destruction or by making another will saying that the earlier will is revoked.

It is necessary for the testator to appoint an **executor** who will wind up the estate and pay out the **beneficiaries.** It is best to appoint more than one executor so that no single individual will have a free hand in what can be a very powerful position.

Unless a will is made with marriage in mind and is intended to survive the marriage, it is automatically revoked when the testator marries. In Scotland, a will is automatically revoked by the subsequent birth of a child. In the **interpretation** of wills, outside **evidence** can be brought in to help a **judge** gauge the testator's intention—but only if the words are ambiguous. Wherever possible a judge will aim to avoid cancelling a will on the grounds of ambiguity since the testator obviously intended a will to exist.

Standard will forms are available from stationers but they give little advice on wording and are usually suitable only for drawing up a simple will.

The cost of getting a **solicitor** to draw up a will is likely to be repaid by tax savings and by avoiding complications later.

Wills need not be full of hereofs, **thereofs** and **whereofs**. Apart from using a few necessary **terms of art,** solicitors should be capable, at no extra cost, of drafting a will in normal English.

In the past, wills have ended with a wordy *attestation clause* to be read and signed by the witnesses: *Signed by the above-named as his last will in the presence of us present at the same time who at his request in his presence and in the presence of each other have hereunto subscribed our names as witnesses.* Something a little crisper is now gaining favour: *Signed by the above-named in our presence and then by us in his.*

See **intestacy; last will and testament.**

winding-up order

A **court** order compulsorily winding up a company in response to a **petition** from a **creditor** or a company member who is liable to contribute to the assets if winding-up takes place. The usual reason for granting the order is that the company is insolvent, which usually means that it cannot pay its debts. But petitions can be obtained against thoroughly solvent companies. For example, a creditor may present a petition if he or she is owed more than £750, has demanded payment and has gone more than 3 weeks without satisfaction. Vast numbers of petitions are withdrawn when such debts are settled.

See **liquidator.**

wingers

Those on either side of the chairman or chairwoman when three **magistrates** sit on the **bench**.

with costs

A **statement** added to a **court** order which shows that the **costs** of the **case** have been awarded to the winner—the loser pays.

without prejudice

A phrase often used in the headings of **solicitors'** letters to show that the contents of the letter cannot be used as **evidence** in any future **court** proceedings without the consent of both sides. It is short for *without prejudice to the question in dispute.* The aim is to allow negotiations to occur freely without any admission of liability.

witness

1 Someone who signs a document to prove that he or she was present when others signed it.

2 Someone who gives **evidence** in **court** or, sometimes, by **affidavit**.

witnesseth

To give formal **evidence** of. The -th ending in the present tense third person has dropped out of popular usage, existing in speech only when people quote the King James version of the Bible. But *Now this deed witnesseth* is often found in documents drafted by old-fashioned **solicitors**—and modern solicitors using old-fashioned **formbooks**. Solicitors can either omit the whole phrase or say *This deed witnesses.*

wounding

Breaking of the skin or of a membrane such as the lips—a bruise is not enough to constitute wounding. This is one of the **offences** termed **assault**. *Malicious wounding* means there was an intention to commit the act or recklessness about it. Serious offences of wounding can lead to **sentences** from three years to **life imprisonment**. Wounding with a broken glass or bottle (*glassing*) is likely to attract at least a 3-year sentence. **Courts** also take a dim view of kicking or stamping on a victim's head, where a sentence of 4 years would be likely.

writ

1 A document which begins many forms of **civil action** in the **High Court**.

2 A **court** order directing someone to act or to cease acting in a certain way.

3 In Scotland, a document indicating **title**.

wrongful dismissal

The ending of a **contract** of employment in a way that breaks the contract. An employee who is wrongfully dismissed can claim **damages** in **court**.

See **unfair dismissal**.

Y

youth court
  See **juvenile court**.

youth offender institutions
  Places where offenders aged 15–21 can be detained after
  sentence. They have replaced borstal training and
  imprisonment.

Z

zebra crossing

A road crossing for pedestrians, marked out by black and white stripes on the road and yellow flashing globes at each end. It gives precedence to pedestrians actually on the crossing; it is an **offence** to park or overtake within the area marked by zigzag lines on the approach to a zebra crossing.

See **Pelican crossing.**